The Talmud
of the
Land of Israel

Chicago Studies in the History of Judaism
Edited by Jacob Neusner

The University of Chicago Press
Chicago and London

The Talmud of the Land of Israel

A Preliminary Translation and Explanation

Volume 30   Baba Batra

Translated by   Jacob Neusner

Jacob Neusner is University Professor and Ungerleider Distinguished Scholar of Judaic Studies at Brown University. He is the author of numerous works, including *Judaism: The Evidence of the Mishnah*, published by the University of Chicago Press.

The University of Chicago Press, Chicago 60637
The University of Chicago Press, Ltd., London

© 1984 by The University of Chicago
All rights reserved. Published 1984
Printed in the United States of America
91 90 89 88 87 86 85 84   5 4 3 2 1

Publication of this volume has been supported by a grant from the Max Richter Foundation.

Library of Congress Cataloging in Publication Data

Talmud Yerushalmi. English. 1982.
  The Talmud of the land of Israel.

  (Chicago studies in the history of Judaism)
  Includes bibliographies and indexes.
  1. Talmud Yerushalmi—Commentaries. I. Neusner, Jacob, 1932–   . II. Title. III. Series.
BM498.5.E5 1982   296.1′2407   81-13115
ISBN 0-226-57619-1 (set)
      0-226-57690-6 (vol. 30)

For
The Zuckerman Family

Alan S. Zuckerman
Roberta Brenner Zuckerman
Gregory S. Zuckerman
Ezra W. Zuckerman
Shara O. Zuckerman

Contents

Foreword

This translation into English of the Talmud of the Land of Israel ("Palestinian Talmud," "Yerushalmi") is preliminary and provisional, even though it is not apt to be replaced for some time. It is preliminary, first, because a firm and final text for translation is not in hand; second, because a modern commentary of a philological and *halakhic* character is not yet available; and, third, because even the lower criticism of the text has yet to be undertaken. Consequently, the meanings imputed to the Hebrew and Aramaic words and the sense ascribed to them in this translation at best are merely a first step. When a systematic effort at the lower criticism of the extant text has been completed, a complete philological study and modern dictionary along comparative lines made available, and a commentary based on both accomplished, then the present work will fall away, having served for the interim. Unhappily, as I said, that interim is apt to be protracted. Text-critics, lexicographers, and exegetes are not apt to complete their work on Yerushalmi within this century.

The purpose of this preliminary translation is to make possible a set of historical and religions-historical studies on the formation of Judaism in the Land of Israel from the closure of the Mishnah to the completion of the Talmud of the Land of Israel and the time of the composition of the first *midrashic* compilations. Clearly, no historical, let alone religions-historical, work can be contemplated without a theory of the principal document and source for the study, the Palestinian Talmud. No theory can be attempted, however tentative and provisional, without a complete, prior statement of what the document appears to wish to say and how its materials seem to have come to closure. It follows that the natural next steps, beyond my now-finished history of Mishnaic law and account of the Judaism revealed in that history, carry us to the present project. Even those steps, when they are taken, will have to be charted with all due regard to the pitfalls of a translation which is preliminary, based upon a text which as yet has not been subjected even to the clarifying exercises of lower criticism. Questions will have to be shaped appropriate to the parlous state of the evidence. But even if the historical and religions-historical program were to be undertaken in the Hebrew language instead of in English, those who might wish to carry on inquiries into the history of the Jews and of Judaism in the land of Israel in the third and fourth centuries would face precisely the same task we do. No one can proceed without a systematic account of the evidence and a theory of how the evidence may and may not be utilized. Further explanation of the plan and execution of this work will be found in volume 34, pp. x–xiv.

It remains only to thank those who helped with this volume. My student, Mr. Roger Brooks, checked my translation against the Leiden manuscript and the *editio princeps* and saved me a great deal of tedious work in so doing. He looked up all the biblical verses in this tractate, and also uncovered more than a few points requiring attention and correction. I am grateful for his hard and careful work. Professor Richard Sarason of Hebrew Union College served as the critical reader for this volume. I am thankful for the many corrections and observations supplied by him and, still more, for his willingness to take time out to study this tractate and so improve my work on it. I retain full responsibility for whatever unsolved problems and deficiencies may remain. The Abbreviations, Bibliography, and Glossary at the end of the present volume were prepared with the help of Professor Alan J. Avery-Peck. Mrs. Marie Louise Murray typed the entire manuscript and did so with unusual care and a high standard of accuracy. She also contributed corrections of various details. Miss Winifred Bell did some additional typing. I could not have done this work without the help of these loyal co-workers.

Baba Batra

Introduction to Baba Batra

The concluding tractate in the triplet on civil law cannot be differentiated from its predecessor, since Mishnah Baba Batra begins right in the middle of a topical unit inaugurated at the end of Mishnah Baba Mesia. Once the theme of real estate transactions is concluded, the tractate goes on to commercial transactions and then legal documents, with special attention to wills and bonds of indebtedness.

Scripture supplies the principles realized in the law. For the present tractate, however, Scripture provides remarkably few facts. The relevant biblical passages are as follows:

Lev. 19:35–36:

You shall do no wrong in judgment, in measures of length or weight or quantity. You shall have just balances, just weights, a just *ephah*, and a just *hin*: I am the Lord your God, who brought you out of the land of Egypt.

Deut. 25:13–16:

You shall not have in your bag two kinds of weights, a large and a small. You shall not have in your house two kinds of measures, a large and a small. A full and just weight you shall have, a full and just measure you shall have; that your days may be prolonged in the land which the Lord your God gives you. For all who do such things, all who act dishonestly, are an abomination to the Lord your God.

Numbers 27:8–11:

And you shall say to the people of Israel: If a man dies, and has no son, then you shall cause his inheritance to pass to his daughter. And if he has no daughter, then you shall give his inheritance to his brothers. And if he has no brothers, then you shall give his inheritance to his father's brothers. And if his father has no brothers, then you shall give his inheritance to his kinsman that is next to him of his family, and he shall possess it. And it shall be to the people of Israel a statute and an ordinance, as the Lord commanded Moses.

Deut. 21:15–17:

If a man has two wives, the one loved and the other disliked, and they have borne him children, both the loved and the disliked, and if the firstborn son is hers that is disliked, then on the day when he assigns his possessions as an inheritance to his sons, he may not treat the son of the loved as the firstborn in preference to the son of the disliked, who is the firstborn, but he shall acknowledge the firstborn, the son of the disliked, by giving him a double portion of all that he has, for he is the first issue of his strength; the right of the firstborn is his.

The topical structure of this tractate cannot be understood except in relation to its two predecessors, for Baba Qamma, Baba Mesia, and Baba Batra form a single continuous discourse on civil law. That is why at the beginning of our study of this tractate, as at the start of volumes 28 and 29, we must take account of all three tractates. Now when we do survey the three Babas together, what we see is a simple set of eight units. These move from abnormal events (units **I–IV**) to normal ones (units **V–VIII**). They begin with damages done by chattels or by a human being, thefts, and other sorts of misappropriation of the property of others, with special attention to how we restore to a state of normality the property and person of the injured party. This large unit runs through the whole of Baba Qamma and into the middle of Baba Mesia, down through M. B.M. 5:11. The second half of the three tractates covers normal events—labor relationships; rentals and bailments; then a huge unit on real estate transactions; and, finally, attention to inheritances and estates. That the intent is to produce two complementary constructions, covering what we may call, generally, abnormal or illicit, then generally normal or licit, transactions, is shown by the correspondence of unit **IV**, illicit commercial transactions (overcharge and usury), and unit **VII**, licit commercial transactions (the legal transfer of goods, unstipulated conditions and how they are enforced). This overall plan may also explain why we have two distinct treatments of bailments, **III.** C, on damages to bailments, and **V.** C, E, on the responsibilities of the bailee. Let us now survey the entire sequence of the three tractates.

BABA QAMMA

I. Damage by Chattels (1:1–6:6)

A. *The fundamental rules of assessing damages when the cause is one's property, animate and inanimate. The ox. 1:1–2:6*

1:1   There are four generative causes of damages: ox, pit, crop-destroying beast, and fire. While they differ, they have in common the trait that they do damage and one is responsible for what they do.

1:2   In the case of anything of which I am liable to take care, I am deemed to render possible whatever damage it may do—in whole or in part. Exceptions: property held by the cult, not held by Israelites, not actually owned, and what is located in the domain of the defendant (whose property has caused the damage).

1:3   Assessment of compensation for injury is in terms of ready cash, but it is paid in kind.

1:4   These five are deemed harmless (so that, if they do damage, the owner pays only half damages, with liability limited to the value of the carcass of the ox which did the damage), and these five are deemed attested dangers (so that liability is unlimited by the value of the ox which did the damage). In general: a beast is not regarded as an attested danger in regard to butting, pushing, biting, lying down, or kicking. The tooth is an attested danger to eat whatever is suitable for eating, and the like.

2:1   *Exposition of M. 1:4:* How is *the leg* deemed an attested danger in regard to breaking something as it walks along?

2:2   *Exposition of M. 1:4:* How is *the tooth* deemed an attested danger in regard to eating what is suitable for eating?

2:3   The dog or goat which jumped from the top of the roof and broke utensils—the owner pays full damages, because they are attested dangers. If the dog took a cake which had a cinder attached and ate the cake and set fire to grain, for the cake the owner pays full damages, and for the standing grain, half. The former is what the dog is liable to do, the latter is unusual.

2:4 What sort of animal is deemed harmless, and what is one which is an attested danger? The procedure for declaring a beast an attested danger.

2:5 *Exposition of M. 1:4:* An ox which causes damage in the domain of the one who is injured is liable—how so? If it happened in public domain, the owner pays half damages, but if it was in the domain of the injured party, he pays full damages.

2:6 Man is perpetually deemed to be an attested danger, under all circumstances.

B. *Damages done in the public domain.* 3:1–3:7

3:1 He who leaves a jug in the public domain and someone else came and stumbled on it and broke it—the latter is exempt. If the jug did damage, the one who left it there is liable.

3:2–3 He who pours water into the public domain, and someone else was injured on it, is liable. Five-part constructions makes the single point that one who creates a hazard in the public domain is liable for damages.

3:4 Two pot sellers going along in single file, the first stumbled and fell and the second stumbled over the first—the first is liable to compensate the second for his injuries. He did not warn the other.

3:5 This one comes with his jar, and that with his beam—if this one's jar was broken by that one's beam, the owner of the beam is exempt, for he had every right to walk along where he did, just as did the other.

3:6 Two going along in the public domain, one running, the other ambling, or both running, and they injured one another—both exempt. Both have every right to be there.

3:7 He who chops wood in private property and the chips injured someone in the public domain, or contrariwise, is liable.

C. *Exercises and illustrations on the ox.* 3:8–4:4

3:8 The oxen generally deemed harmless which injured one another—the owner pays half damages of the excess of the value of the injury done by the less injured to the more injured ox. If both were attested dangers, the owner pays full damages for the excess. Further exercises on the interplay between the one deemed harmless and the one which was an attested danger.

3:9   Meir and Judah on the interpretation and application of Exod. 21:35.

3:10 There is he who is liable for the deed of his ox and exempt on account of his own deed or exempt for the deed of his ox and liable on account of his own deed. The principles illustrated are that man inflicts humiliation, but oxen do not; that the rule of Exod. 21:26–27 applies to the owner, not to the beast; and that one is not liable for the death penalty and for damages simultaneously.

3:11 A triplet which uses the facts of this unit to illustrate the proposition that the one who lays claim against his fellow bears the burden of proof.

4:1   An ox deemed harmless which gored four or five oxen, one after the other—the owner pays compensation to the last among them, then to the next-to-the-last, and so on.

4:2   An ox which is an attested danger as to its own species, but not an attested danger as to what is not its own species—for that for which it is an attested danger, the owner pays full damages, and for that for which it is not an attested danger, he pays half damages.

4:3   An ox of an Israelite which gored an ox belonging to the sanctuary—the owner is exempt, since Exod. 21:35 excludes oxen belonging to the sanctuary. The same is so for a gentile. Illustrated: M. 1:2.

4:4   An ox of a person of sound senses which gored an ox belonging to a deaf-mute, idiot, or minor—the owner is liable. But one belonging to a deaf-mute, idiot, or minor which gored an ox belonging to a person of sound senses—the former is exempt. Procedure for declaring an ox belonging to a deaf-mute, etc., to be attested danger.

D. *The ransom and the death penalty for the ox.* 4:5–5:4

4:5   An ox which gored a man who died—if it was an attested danger, the owner pays the ransom price. If it was deemed harmless, he is exempt.

4:6   An ox which was rubbing itself against a wall, and the wall fell on a man—if it had intended to kill another beast and killed a man, etc., the ox is exempt.

4:7   An ox belonging to a woman, an estate, a guardian, etc.,—these oxen are liable to the death penalty.

4:8   An ox which goes forth to be stoned and which the owner declared to be sanctified is not sanctified, and if the meat is properly slaughtered, it is nonetheless prohibited. But if this was before the court process was complete, it is sanctified, the meat is permitted.

4:9   If one handed an ox to a bailee, the bailee takes the place of the owner.

5:1   An ox deemed harmless which gored a cow, and a newborn calf was found dead beside her, so we do not know whether or not the ox killed the calf—the owner pays half damages for the cow, and quarter damages for the calf.

5:2-3   The potter who brought his pots into the courtyard of a householder without permission, and the beast of the householder broke them—the householder is exempt. If the beast was injured on them, the owner of the pots is liable. If the householder gave permission, however, he bears liability.

5:4   An ox intending to gore its fellow which hit a woman and caused a miscarriage—the owner of the ox is exempt from paying compensation for the offspring.

E. *Damages done by the pit* (M. 1:1). 5:5-7

5:5   He who digs a pit in private domain and opens it into public domain, or in public domain and opens it into private, or in private and opens it into private, is liable for damage done by the pit.

5:6   A pit belonging to partners, and one passed it and did not cover it, and the second did likewise—the second is liable.

5:7   All the same are an ox and all other beasts so far as falling into a pit (and various other biblical references to an ox) are concerned. Why is an ox specified?

F. *Crop-destroying beast* (M. 1:1). 6:1-3

6:1-2   He who brought a flock into a fold and shut the gate properly, but the flock got out and did damages, is exempt. If he did not shut the gate properly, he is liable.

6:3   He who stacks sheaves in the field of his fellow without permission and the beast of the owner of the field ate them—the owner of the field is exempt. (Cf. M. 5:20.)

G. *Damages done by fire* (M. 1:1). 6:4-6

6:4   He who causes a fire to break out through the action of a deaf-mute, etc.

6:5   He who sets fire to a stack of grain, in which utensils were located—Judah: the one who lit the fire pays compensation for whatever was in the stack which burned up. Sages: only for the stack of wheat.

6:6   A spark which flew out from under the hammer and did damage—the smith is liable.

II. Damages Done by Persons. Theft (7:1–10:10)

A. *Penalties for the theft of an ox or a sheep, in line with Ex. 22:1-4.*

7:1   More encompassing is the rule covering payment for twofold restitution than the rule covering payment of fourfold or fivefold restitution.

7:2   If one stole an ox or sheep on the evidence of two witnesses and was convicted of having slaughtered or sold it on the basis of their testimony, or on the basis of the testimony of two other witnesses, he pays fourfold or fivefold restitution. If he stole or sold an ox or sheep on the Sabbath, etc., he pays fourfold or fivefold restitution.

7:3   If he stole an ox or sheep on the evidence of two witnesses and slaughtered or sold it on the basis of their testimony, and they turned out to be false witnesses, they pay full restitution.

7:4   If one stole on the evidence of two and was accused of having slaughtered or sold the ox or sheep on the basis of only one witness, he pays twofold restitution but not fourfold or fivefold restitution.

7:5   If one sold all but one hundredth part of the stolen ox or sheep, he pays twofold restitution but not fourfold or fivefold restitution.

7:6   If the sheep was dragging a sheep or an ox but it died in the domain of the owner, he is exempt. If he lifted it up or removed it from the domain of the owner and then it died, he is liable.

[7:7   They do not rear small cattle in the Land of Israel, but they do so in Syria and in the wastelands which are in the Land of Israel.]

B. *Penalties for assault.* 8:1–7

8:1   He who inflicts injury on his fellow is liable for compensation on five counts: injury, pain, medical costs, loss of income, and indignity.

8:2   Continuation of foregoing.

8:3   He who hit his father or mother but did not make a wound, etc., is liable on all counts.

8:4   A deaf-mute, an idiot, and a minor—meeting up with them is a bad thing. He who injured them is liable, but they who injured other people are exempt.

8:5   He who hit his father or mother and did make a wound is exempt, because he is tried for his life.

8:6   He who boxed the ear of his fellow pays a *sela*; if he smacked him, he pays two hundred *zuz*; with the back of his hand, four hundred *zuz*.

8:7   Even though the defendant pays off the plaintiff, he still has to seek forgiveness. If one says, "Blind my eye," the one who does so still is liable.

C. *Penalties for damages to property. Restoring what is stolen.*
    9:1–10:1

9:1   He who steals wood and makes it into utensils pays compensation in accord with the value of the wood at the time of the theft.

9:2   If he stole a beast and it got old, he pays compensation in accord with the value at the time of the theft.

9:3   If he gave something to a craftsman to repair and the object was spoiled, the craftsman is liable to pay compensation.

9:4   He who hands over wool to a dyer and the dye in the cauldron burned the wool—the dyer pays the value of the wool.

9:5   He who stole something from his fellow worth a *perutah* and took an oath that he had stolen nothing and then wants to make restitution must take the object to him, even all the way to Media.

9:6   If the thief paid back the principal but not the added fifth, he need not do so. If he paid back the added fifth but not the principal, he needs to do so.

9:7   If he paid back the principal but swore falsely about the added fifth and then confessed, he has to pay back an added fifth on the added fifth.

9:8   If a person denied having a bailment and takes an oath falsely and then witnesses testify that the oath was false, he pays twofold restitution. Had he confessed on his own, he would have had to pay back the principal, an added fifth, and a guilt offering.

9:9–10   He who steals from his father and takes an oath to him (that he did not do so), and then the father dies, pays back the principal and added fifth to the other sons or brothers.

9:11   He who steals from a proselyte and takes an oath to him and then the proselyte dies—lo, this one pays the principal and added fifth to the priests, in line with Num. 5:8.

9:12   If he had paid over the money to the men of the priestly watch on duty and then died, the heirs cannot retrieve the funds from the priests, since it is said Num. 5:10.

10:1   He who steals food and gives it to his children—they are exempt from making restitution.

10:2   If tax collectors took one's ass and gave him another, lo, it is his, because the original owners have given up hope of getting it back.

10:3   He who recognizes his utensils or books in someone else's possession and a report of theft had circulated—the purchaser takes an oath to him specifying how much he had paid the thief, then the original owner pays that price and retrieves his property.

10:4   If one suffered a loss to help someone else save his property, he can claim only wages, unless he had established a prior condition for compensation for his loss.

10:5   He who stole a field from his fellow, and bandits seized it from him—if it was a blow from which the whole district suffered, he may say to the original victim, "Lo, there is yours before you."

10:6   He who stole or borrowed something from his fellow, or with whom the latter deposited something in a settled area, may not return it to him in the wilderness.

10:7   He who says to his fellow, "I have stolen from you, and I don't know whether I returned the object or not," is liable to pay restitution.

10:8   He who steals a lamb from a flock and returned it and the lamb died or was stolen again is liable to make it up.

10:9   They do not purchase from herdsmen wool, milk, or kids, since these are likely to have been stolen from the owner of the flock.

10:10 Shreds of wool which the laundryman pulls out belong to him. Those which the woolcomber pulls out belong to the householder.

BABA MESIA

III. The Disposition of Other Peoples' Possessions
(1:1–3:12)

A. *Conflicting claims on lost objects.* 1:1–4

1:1–2   Two lay hold of a cloak—both take an oath and they divide it. If one party concedes the claim to the other for part, only the other part, not conceded, is subject to an oath.

1:3–4   If one was riding on a beast and saw a lost object and said to his fellow, "Give it to me," but the other took it and said, "I take possession of it"—the latter has acquired possession of it.

B. *Returning an object to the original owner.* 1:5–2:1

1:5   Things found by someone's dependents belong to him. Things not found by his dependents do not.

1:6–8   If one found bonds of indebtedness, he should (not) return them. Lists of commercial papers and documents not to be returned.

2:1–2   What lost items are the finder's, and which ones is he liable to proclaim (seeking the owner)?

2:3–4   If one found pigeons tied together behind a fence, he should not touch them. If there is evidence that an object belongs to someone, it should not be touched.

2:5   Exegesis of Deut. 22:2: Everything that has distinctive marks and that is subject to a claim must be returned to the owner.

2:6   And for how long is one liable to make proclamation of having found an object?

2:7   If a claimant has described what he has lost but has not specified distinctive marks, one should not give it to him.

2:8   Taking care of objects one has found, pending return to the rightful owner.

2:9   What is lost property (which must be returned)?

2:10   The limits of one's responsibility to retrieve an animal and return it to the owner.

2:11   If one has to choose between seeking what he has lost and what his father has lost, his own takes precedence.

C. *Rules of bailment.* 3:1–12

3:1   He who deposits a beast or utensils with his fellow, and they were stolen, if the bailee made restitution and was unwilling to take an oath, and the thief was found, he pays restitution to the bailee. If not, then to the owner.

3:2   He who rents a cow from his fellow and then lent it to someone else, and it died of natural causes, the one who rented it takes an oath that it died of natural causes, and the one who borrowed it pays compensation.

3:3–5   If one said to two people, "The father of one of you deposited money with me, and I don't know which one it was," he pays a *maneh* to each of them, for he has admitted it on his own. Two further cases of bailment where there is a conflicting claim.

3:6   He who deposits produce with his fellow—even if it is going to waste, the fellow should not touch it.

3:7–8   He who deposits produce with his fellow—the bailee when returning it may make reductions due to natural depletion or the
action of mice.

3:9   He who deposits a jar with his fellow, and the owner did not
specify a place for it, and it was moved and broken . . .

3:10   He who deposits coins with his fellow, if the latter did not tend
to them properly, he is responsible. He did not take care of them
in the ordinary way. If he did, he is not liable to make them up.

3:11   He who deposits coins with a money changer.

3:12   He who makes use of a bailment: assessing compensation.

IV. Illicit Commercial Transactions (4:1–5:11)

A. *Overcharge and misrepresentation.* 4:1–12

4:1–2   Coins do not acquire commodities, but commodities do acquire
coins. Gold, a commodity, acquires silver coins. Thus if the
buyer had made acquisition of produce but the coins were not
paid over, the buyer cannot retract.

4:3   Overreaching (fraud) constitutes an overcharge of four pieces of
silver out of twenty-four—one-sixth of the purchase price. How
long may one retract in the case of fraud?

4:4   Both buyer and seller are subject to the rules of fraud.

4:5   How much may a *sela* be defective and still not fall under the
rule of fraud?

4:6   How long is it permitted to return a defective coin?

4:7–8   Defrauding involves an overcharge of four pieces of silver to a
sela, and a claim involving a court-imposed oath, etc. Formal
construction.

4:9   These are matters which are not subject to a claim of fraud on
account of overcharge: slaves, bills of indebtedness, real estate,
and what has been consecrated.

4:10   A claim of fraud applies to the spoken word. One may not say to
a storekeeper, "How much is this object?" when one does not
plan to buy it.

4:11–12 They do not commingle one sort of produce with another sort of produce (and so adulterate what is for sale).

B. *Usury.* 5:1–11

5:1 What is interest, and what is increase?

5:2 He who lends money to his fellow should not live in his court-yard for free.

5:3 If one sold him a field and the buyer paid part of the fee, and the seller said to him, "Whenever you want, bring the rest of the money and then take the field"—such a transaction is forbidden. If one lent money on the security of the field and said, "If you do not pay me by this date three years hence, then it is mine"—it is his.

5:4 They do not set up a storekeeper for half the profit, unless one pays him an additional wage as a worker. Otherwise his free service to the partner constitutes usury.

5:5 They assess and put out for rearing a cow, an ass, or anything which works for its keep for half the profits. The rancher gets the benefit of the animal's labor, so the capitalist does not have to pay for the rancher's service in addition.

5:6 They do not accept from an Israelite a flock on "iron terms," that the one who tends the flock pays a fixed fee and restores the value of the flock as it was when it was handed over to him, because this is interest. There must be an equal sharing in the risks and profits.

5:7 They do not strike a bargain for the price of produce before the market price is announced. This is "increase" (M. 5:1).

5:8–9 A man may lend his tenant farmers wheat to be repaid in wheat if it is for seed, but not if it is for food.

5:10 A man may say to his fellow, "Weed with me, and I'll weed with you," but not, "Weed with me, and I'll hoe with you."

5:11 Those who participate in a loan in interest violate a negative commandment.

V. Hiring Workers. Rentals and Bailments (6:1–8:3)

A. *The mutual obligations of worker and employer.* 6:1–2

6:1–2   He who hired craftsmen and one party deceived the other—one has no claim on the other except a complaint.

B. *Rentals.* 6:3–5

6:3   He who rented out an ass to drive it through hill country but drove it through the valley, or vice versa, and the ass died, is liable.

6:4–5   He who hired a cow to plow in the hill country but plowed in the valley, if the plowshare was broken, is exempt. If he hired the cow to plow in the valley and plowed in the hill country, if the plowshare was broken, he is liable.

C. *Bailments.* 6:6–6:8

6:6   All craftsmen are in the status of paid bailees. But any who said, "Take what is yours and pay me," enters the status of an unpaid bailee.

6:7   If one made a loan and took a pledge, he is in the status of a paid bailee of the pledge.

6:8   The bailee who moves a jar from one place to another and broke it, whether unpaid or paid, must take an oath (that the jar was broken by accident).

D. *The mutual obligations of worker and employer.* 7:1–7

7:1   He who hires day workers and tells them to start work early or stay late—in a place in which that is not the custom, he has no right to do so.

7:2–3   And these have the right to eat the produce on which they are working, a right endowed by the Torah.

7:4   If the laborer was working on figs, he has not got the right to eat grapes.

7:5   A worker has the right to eat cucumbers, even to a *denar*'s worth, or dates, even to a *denar*'s worth.

7:6   A man makes a deal with the householder not to exercise his right to eat produce on which he is working, in behalf of himself or other adults, but not in behalf of dependents.

7:7   He who hires workers to work in his fourth-year plantings—lo, these do not have the right to eat. If he did not tell them in advance about the character of the crop, he has to provide food for them.

E. *Bailments.* 7:8–8:3

7:8   There are four kinds of watchmen: unpaid bailee, borrower, paid bailee, hirer. Unpaid bailee takes an oath in all cases; borrower pays in all circumstances of damages to a bailment; paid bailee and hirer take an oath.

7:9–11   A single wolf does not count as an unavoidable accident; two do (and the paid bailee and hirer do not have to pay in the latter case).

8:1   He who borrowed a cow and borrowed the service of its owner with it and the cow died—the borrower is exempt.

8:2   He who borrowed a cow, borrowed it for half a day and hired it for half a day, etc., and the cow died—the lender claims, "The borrowed cow died," or, "At the time it was borrowed, it died," and the borrower says, "I don't know,"—the borrower is liable (as at M. B.M. 1:1).

8:3   He who borrowed a cow and the one who lent it sent it along with his son, slave, or a messenger, and the cow died—the borrower is exempt, for it had not yet reached the domain of the borrower.

VI. Real Estate (B.M. 8:4–10:6, B.B. 1:1–5:5)

A. *Prologue.* 8:4–5

8:4   He who exchanges a cow for an ass, and the cow produces offspring—this one says, "It was before I made the sale," and that one says, "It was after I made the purchase"—let them divide the proceeds. Also: purchase of two fields, one big, one small.

8:5   He who sells olive trees for firewood and before they are chopped down they produce a small quantity of fruit—lo,

this belongs to the owner of the olive trees (not to the landowner). Conflicting claims (as above).

B. *Landlord-tenant relations.* 8:3–9

8:6   He who rents a house to his fellow without a lease in the rainy
season has not got the right to evict him from the Festival to
Passover.

8:7   He who leases a house to his fellow is liable to provide a door,
bolt, and lock, and anything made by a craftsman, but the one
to whom the house has been leased can provide anything not
made by a craftsman.

8:8   He who leases a house to his fellow for a year—if the year is
intercalated, it is intercalated to the advantage of the tenant. If it
is rented by the month, it is intercalated to the advantage of the
landlord.

8:9   He who leased a house to his fellow, and the house fell down, is
liable to provide him with another house of the same character.

C. *The landlord's relations with a tenant farmer and sharecropper.*
9:1–10

9:1   He who leases a field from his fellow, in a place in which it is the
custom to cut the crops—he must cut them. If it is the custom
to uproot them, he must uproot them.

9:2   He who leases a field from his fellow which is irrigated or an
orchard—if the water source went dry, or the trees were cut
down, the tenant may not deduct the damages from the rental.

9:3   He who as a sharecropper leases a field from his fellow and then
neglected the field—they make an estimate of how much the
field is suitable to produce, and the tenant pays that.

9:4   He who leases a field from his fellow and did not want to weed
it—they pay no attention to his claim.

9:5   He who leases a field from his fellow and it did not produce a
crop still has to tend it.

9:6   He who leases a field from his fellow and locusts ate it up—if it
was a disaster affecting the entire province, he may deduct the
damages from his rental.

9:7   He who leases a field from his fellow in return for ten *kors* of wheat a year, and the field was smitten and produced poor quality grain—the tenant pays him off from produce grown in that field anyhow.

9:8   He who leases a field from his fellow to sow barley in it may not sow it with wheat.

9:9   He who leases a field from his fellow for a period of only a few years may not sow it with flax.

9:10   He who leases a field from his fellow "for one septannate" at the rate of seven hundred *zuz*—the Seventh Year counts in the number of years. If he leased it from him for seven years, it does not.

D. *Miscellanies: Paying laborers promptly. Taking a pledge.*
   9:11–13

9:11   A day worker collects his wage any time of the night, and a night worker by day.

9:12   The fee owing for a worker, a beast, or a utensil must be paid promptly.

9:13   He who lends money to his fellow should exact a pledge from him only in court.

E. *Joint holders of a common property.* B.M. 10:1–6, B.B. 1:1–6

10:1   A house and an upper story belonging to two people—if it fell down, they divide the ruins.

10:2   A house and an upper story belonging to two people—if the floor of the upper room was broken and the householder does not want to repair it—lo, the owner of the upper story goes and lives downstairs.

10:3   A house and an upper story belonging to two people which fell down—if the resident of the upper story told the householder to rebuild but he does not want to rebuild, lo, the resident of the upper story rebuilds the lower story and lives there.

10:4   So too an olive-press built into a rock.

10:5   He whose wall was near the garden of his fellow and it fell down, and the owner of the garden said to him, "Clear out your stones," but the other said to him, "They're yours"—they pay no attention to him.

10:6   Two terraced gardens, one above the other, with vegetables between them—Meir: they belong to the garden on top; Judah: to the one on the bottom.

BABA BATRA

1:1   Joint holders to a courtyard who wanted to make a partition in the courtyard build the wall down the middle.

1:2   So is the rule in the case of a garden.

1:3   He whose land surrounds that of his fellow on three sides and who made a fence on those sides—they do not require the other party to share in the expense. If the other party completed the fourth wall, they do.

1:4   The wall of a courtyard which fell down—they require each partner in the courtyard to help rebuild it.

1:5   They force a joint holder in the courtyard to contribute to the building of a gatehouse and a door for the courtyard.

1:6   They do not divide up a courtyard unless there will be an area of four cubits by four for each party.

F. *Not infringing the property rights of others.* 2:1–4

2:1   One may not dig a cistern near that of his fellow.

2:2   A person should not set up an oven in a room unless there is a space of four cubits above it.

2:3   A person should not open a bakeshop or dyer's shop under the grain store of his neighbor.

2:4   He whose wall is near the wall of his fellow may not build another wall near it unless he sets it four cubits back.

2:5   They set up a ladder four cubits from the dovecote of one's neighbor, so that the marten will not jump into the dovecote.

2:6   A fallen pigeon which is found within fifty cubits—lo, it belongs to the owner of the dovecote.

4:5   He who sells an olive-press has sold the vat but not the pressing boards.

4:6   He who sells a bathhouse has not sold the boards.

4:7   He who sells a town has sold the houses but not the movables.

4:8   He who sells a field has sold the stones.

4:9   But he has not sold . . .

5:1   He who sells a ship has sold the mast . . . , but not the slaves.

5:2   He who sells an ass has not sold its trappings.

5:3   He who sells an ass has sold the foal.

5:4   He who buys two trees in his fellow's field has not bought the ground on which they are growing.

5:5   He who sells the head of a large beast has not sold the feet.

VII. Licit Commercial Transactions (5:6–7:4)

A. *Conditions of irrevocable transfer of goods.* 5:6–11

5:6   Rules for those who sell: If one has sold wheat as good and it turns out to be bad, the purchaser can retract. If it was sold as bad and turns out to be good, the seller can retract. If it was sold as bad and is bad, neither can retract.

5:7   He who sells produce to his fellow—if the buyer drew it but did not measure it, he has acquired possession of it. If he measured it but did not draw it, he has not acquired possession.

5:8   He who sells wine or oil to his fellow, and the price rose or fell, if this took place before the measure belonging to the purchaser has been filled up, the price advantage goes to the seller.

5:9   He who sends his child to the storekeeper with a *pondion* in his hand—liability for loss.

5:10–11   A wholesaler must clean off his measures once in thirty days, a householder once every twelve months, a storekeeper weekly.

B. *Unstated stipulations in commercial transactions.* 6:1–7:4

6:1   He who sells produce to his fellow and the grain did not sprout is not liable to make it up. He can claim it was food.

6:2   He who sells produce to his fellow—lo, the buyer must agree to accept a certain proportion in spoilage.

6:3   He who sold wine to his fellow, which went sour, is not liable to make it up. But if it was known that this would happen, then it is a purchase made in error and null.

6:4   He who sells a piece of property to his fellow for building a house—the contractor must build it at least four by six, so Aqiba. Ishmael: That is too small, it must be six by eight.

6:5–6   He who has a cistern behind his fellow's house goes in when people usually go in and goes out when people usually go out.

6:7   He who had a public way passing through his field . . .

6:8   He who sells a piece of property to his fellow for a family grave—the contractor makes it in the given dimensions, for a given number of holes.

7:1   He who says to his fellow, "I am selling you a *kor*'s area of arable land"—if there were crevices ten handbreadths deep, etc., they are not included in the measurement of the area. If he said, "Approximately . . . ," then they are included.

7:2   If he said, "A *kor*'s area I am selling, measured by a rope," if he gave any less, the purchaser may deduct the difference.

7:3   If he said, "I am selling you a *kor*'s area, measured by a rope, whether less or more," one expression nullifies the other.

7:4   If he said, "Half a field I sell to you"—they divide the field into portions of equal value.

VIII. Inheritances and Wills. Other Commercial and Legal Documents (8:1–10:8)

A. *Inheritance.* 8:1–9:10

8:1   There are those who inherit and bequeath, do one but not the other, and do neither.

8:2   The order of the passing of an inheritance is thus Num. 27:8

8:3   The daughters of Zelophehad took three portions of the inheritance.

8:4   All the same are the son and the daughter as to matters of inheritance.

8:5   He who says, "My firstborn son will not receive a double portion" has said nothing, for he has made a stipulation contrary to what is written in the Torah. But if one gives away his property, the gift is valid, whatever its character.

8:6   He who says, "This is my son," is believed. If he says, "This is my brother," he is not believed.

8:7   He who writes over his property to his sons has to write, "From today and after death," so Judah. Yosé: He does not.

8:8   If someone left adult and minor children, they divide the estate equally.

9:1   He who died and left sons and daughters—when the estate is large, the sons inherit and the daughters are supported.

9:2   He who left sons and daughters and a child whose sexual traits were not clearly defined—the latter is classed with the females in a large estate, with the males in a small estate.

9:3   If he left adult and minor sons, if the adults improved the value of the estate, the increase is shared by all, unless they stipulated otherwise.

9:4   If one of the brothers fell into public service, the charge or benefit falls to the estate.

9:5   He who sends gifts to his father-in-law's household . . .

9:6   A dying man who wrote over his property to others but left himself a piece of land—his gift is valid.

9:7   He who divides his property by word of mouth . . .

9:8-10   Inheritance in cases of doubt as to the sequence of deaths, e.g., father and son.

   B. *The preparation and confirmation of commercial documents, e.g., writs of debt.* 10:1-6

10:1-2   Unfolded and folded documents: how they are prepared and witnessed.

10:3-4   They write out a writ of divorce for a man even though his wife is not present, and a quittance for the wife, even though the husband is not present. Various other rules for scribes on preparing documents and payment of the scribal fee.

10:5   He who paid part of a debt which he owed and who deposited
        the bond with a third party . . .

10:6   He whose writ of indebtedness was blotted out but who had
        witnesses to confirm what was in it . . .

        C. *Concluding miscellanies.* 10:7–8

10:7   Two brothers, one poor, one rich, whose father left them a bath-
        house or an olive-press. Two men who have identical names and
        the disposition of bonds for each. He who admits one of his
        bonds has been paid off but does not know which one. Collect-
        ing a debt from the guarantor of the loan.

10:8   He who lends money on the security of a bond of indebtedness
        collects what is owing from mortgaged property; if there are
        only witnesses, he collects from unindentured property; if he has
        the debtor's note of hand, he collects from unindentured prop-
        erty. Ishmael: He who wants to get smart had best get busy with
        commercial law.

We now come to Baba Batra in particular. The layout is simple
and predictable. The first half simply completes the topic undertaken in the preceding tractate, through **VI.H**. Then there are
further units, one on licit commercial transactions, by contrast
to unit **IV**'s special interest in damages done through overcharge
and usury, and, finally, inheritances, wills, and documents. This
last unit at the end pays special attention to bonds of indebtedness. The subdivision of the three units is equally logical, al-
though why one unit must come before or after some other is
not always self-evident. The unit on real estate treats landlord-
tenant relations (B, C) and then relations between joint holders
of a common property (E, F). (Perhaps the intrusion of D between these two units is yet another example of the puzzling
phenomenon of the arrangement of unit **V**.) The final part of
unit **VI** turns to transferring title of real estate through usucaption and through sale. The reason these are treated in the present order, G, H, is that the next unit continues the theme of sale
of property, now with regard to movables rather than to real
estate. So clearly there is a governing principle that we move as
smoothly as we can from one theme to the next, on the one side,
or from one problematic to the next, on the other. In the present

case there is a smooth flow of the governing problematic, transferring ownership from one party to another.

That same consideration then governs the arrangement of unit **VII**, since **VII.A** carries forward **VI.H**. The fact that **VII.B** concludes with attention to the division of a field surely cannot be entirely irrelevant to the choice of the topic to follow, which is matters of inheritance and division of estates. That leaves for the end the issue of documentary evidence of inheritance, including **VII.A**, then commercial documents with special attention to writs of debt, **VIII.B**. It seems to me that if the redactors' intent is to allow for a smooth flow from one major theme to the next, they have wholly succeeded.

I Yerushalmi Baba Batra
Chapter One

1:1

[A] *Joint holders [to a courtyard] who wanted to make a partition in the courtyard*

[B] *build the wall in the middle.*

[C] *In a place in which they are accustomed to build it of unshaped stones, hewn stones, half-bricks, or whole bricks,*

[D] *they build it [of that sort of material].*

[E] *All follows the custom of the province.*

[F] *[If they make it] of unhewn stones,*

[G] *this one contributes [a space of] three handbreadths [of his share of the courtyard], and that one supplies [a space of] three handbreadths.*

[H] *[If they build it] of hewn stones, this one supplies two handbreadths and a half [of space], and that one supplies two handbreadths and a half [of space].*

[I] *[If they build it] of half-bricks, this one supplies two handbreadths [of space], and that one supplies two handbreadths [of space].*

[J] *[If they build it out of] whole bricks, this one supplies a handbreadth and a half, and that one supplies a handbreadth and a half.*

[K] *Therefore if the wall should fall down, the location [on which it had stood] and the stones belong to both parties.*

[**II.**A] [12d] [Since the present rule takes for granted that a division may be effected in any sort of courtyard,] how is it that we have learned elsewhere: *They do not divide up a courtyard unless there will be an area of four cubits by four cubits for this one, and four cubits by four cubits for that one* [M. 1:6A]. [Our rule does not recognize such a qualification.]

[B] [To this evident contradiction between the present rule, as interpreted in the stated supposition at A, and the cited passage] one may reply, there [we deal with a case] in which the two partners do not concur. But here we deal with a case in which both of them concur [so it does not matter whether there is the requisite minimum of space produced for each party to the division, since both parties concur in whatever they will receive].

[C] And even if you maintain that [in the present] instance we deal with a case in which the two parties do not concur, [if] this one wills [a division], they force the other party [to carry out the division]. [If] that one wishes [a division of the courtyard], they force this one to [accept it].

[D] Said R. Yohanan, "They enforce [the will of one party upon both partners] in the case of [the division of] courtyards, but they do not enforce [the will of one party upon both partners] in the case of [the division of] roofs."

[E] R. Nissah contemplated ruling [that this statement of Yohanan, that the will of one party is not imposed upon the other in the case of a division] applies in the case of a courtyard which is located above the roof, but in the case of a roof which is above the courtyard, they do impose [the will of one upon both parties].

[F] R. Yohanan contemplated ruling [that it is in the case of a] courtyard which is above the roof that they impose [the will of one upon both], but in the case of a roof which is above the courtyard, they do not do so. [So Nissah's surmise is contrary to Yohanan's qualification of C.]

M. 1:1A–B set the stage for the fancy construction inaugurated by M.1:1C–D and then fully spelled out at M.1:1F–J, with the proper conclusion made explicit by M.1:1K. The measurements of M.1:1F–J simply take account of the varying breadth

of the building materials and the mortar required for the wall;
M.1 : 1G supposes a wall six handbreadths—a cubit—wide, and
so on down. The Talmud's interest is solely in M. 1 : 1A–B—
that is, the point taken for granted by Mishah. The method is to
contrast the present rule with one presenting a qualification
which is evidently not encompassed by said rule. The secondary
development, E–F, then takes up one of the proposed harmo-
nizing interpretations, D. So the whole is tightly organized and
unfolds within a severely limited frame of logic.

1 : 2   [In Leiden MS and *editio princeps* 1 : 2–3]

[A]   *And so is the rule in the case of a garden:*

[B]   *in a place in which it is customary to build a fence, they [require
      a recalcitrant owner] to do so.*

[C]   *But in a valley, in a place in which it is not customary to build a
      fence, they do not require him to do so.*

[D]   *But if [the other party] wants, he may withdraw inside his own
      portion [of the property] and build it.*

[E]   *And [he places] the facing of the wall outside of [the fence] [on
      the side of the neighbor, so indicating his ownership].*

[F]   *Therefore, if the wall should fall down, the location [on which it
      had stood] and the stones are his.*

[G]   *But if they make it with the consent of both parties,*

[H]   *they build the wall in the middle.*

[I]   *They place the facing of the wall on this side and on that side.*

[J]   *Therefore if the fence should fall down, the location [on which it
      had stood] and the stones belong to both parties.*

[I.A]   It was taught: In the case of a garden [vegetable patch],

[B]   whether *it is a place in which it is customary to build a fence* [cf.
      M1 : 2B], or whether it is a place in which it is not customary to
      build a fence,

[C]   they force [a recalcitrant owner to build a fence if the partner so
      desires].

[D]   But as to a valley, in a place in which it is customary to build a fence, they force [the recalcitrant partner to build a fence], while *in a place in which it is not customary to build a fence,* they do not force [him to participate in the project].

M. 1:2A–F make the point that a person cannot be compelled to contribute to the land needed for, or the costs of, the fence. But one of course may build a fence wholly on his own property, leading to F. If the finished stone is on one side of the fence only, that is a sign that all the ground on the unfinished side of the fence belongs to the owner of that field in which the fence is located. The Talmud clarifies the language of M. 1:2B and C, reading the implications of the latter into the former and so correcting the unclarity of Mishnah's formulation.

1:3   [In Leiden MS and *editio princeps* 1:4–5]

[A]   *He who[se] land surrounds that of his fellow on three sides,*

[B]   *and who made a fence on the first, second, and third sides—*

[C]   *they do not require [the other party to share in the expense of building the walls].*

[D]   *R. Yosé says, "If [the neighbor] went and built a fence on the fourth side, they assign to him [his share in the cost of] all [three other fences]."*

[E]   *The wall of a courtyard which fell down—*

[F]   *they require [each partner in the courtyard] to [help] build it, up to a height of four cubits.*

[G]   *[Each one is] assumed to have given, until one will bring proof that he has not contributed to the cost.*

[H]   *[If the fence was built] four cubits and higher, they do not require [a joint holder in the courtyard to contribute to the expenses].*

[I]   *[If the one who did not contribute] built another wall near [the restored one, planning to roof over the intervening space],*

[J]   *even though he did not [actually] put a roof on it,*

[K]   *they assign him [his share in the cost of the] whole [other wall].*

[L]   *[He is] assumed not to have contributed to the cost, until he will bring proof that he has contributed to the cost.*

[I.A]   [With reference to M. 1 : 3A–C, the neighbor's not being required to share in the expense of building the walls, which the Talmud takes to mean that if the one who built the three walls went and completed the fourth, they would impose the cost-sharing on the neighbor,] R. Huna said, "That [implication is valid] on the condition that it is at the time that he built [the three, that he also built the fourth].

[B]   "Thus if he had built it with stone, he [must build the fourth wall] also with stone [if he wishes to impose half of the cost on the neighbor].

[C]   "But here if he had built it with stone and [later on] he went and built [the fourth wall] with bricks, [so that the wall is not so strong as it should be if it were all of stone,] should he be able to collect [from the neighbor his share of the cost] as if the wall had been built with stone, and then whenever it should fall down, he will rebuild it!?" [Obviously, in Huna's view, that is not possible. Hence his original statement, A–B, must be sound.]

[II.A]   *R. Yosé says, "If the neighbor went and built a fence on the fourth side, they assign to him [his share in the cost of all three other fences]"* [M. 1 : 3D].

[B]   R. Huna said, "They assign to him the amount of the basic [cost] of the walls on the other three sides [not just of the fourth]."

[III.A]   *[The wall of a courtyard which fell down—they require each partner to help build it up to a height of four cubits.]* [This is to] the extent of its height [of four cubits].

[B]   As to its length?

[C]   Said R. Nissa, "The wall of a courtyard is made only to afford protection [privacy] for him [as a measure of the property of the owner, hence there is no specified minimum as to the length of the wall which must be reconstructed]. [It must be such as to block off the view of the other party to the courtyard and so afford privacy.]"

[D]   [That statement would then imply a view contrary to M. 1 : 3J, for] they seem to imply that if he wanted to roof over the space,

he does not do so [since the wall under discussion is not adequate for that purpose]. [Hence there is no basis for saying that
if one did roof over the space between the wall restored by one
party and the new wall built by the other, the latter must share
in the cost of the whole other wall (PM).]

[E]   Said R. Yosé b. R. Bun, "Interpret the rule [to apply to a case in
which one put up a roof by extending it] from the beams [of his
own property, without actually laying it down on the wall built
by the other party, and it is to such a case that the statement at
D would pertain]."

The Talmud systematically works through Mishnah, treating
M. 1:3 A–C at **I**, M. 1:3D at **II**, and M. 1:3Iff. at **III**. Huna
glosses at the first two, and the third, meant to spell out the facts
of the matter, generates a problem to be solved on its own.

1:4   [Leiden MS and *editio princeps* 1:6]

[A]   *They force [a joint-holder in the courtyard to contribute to] the
building of a gatehouse and a door for the courtyard.*

[B]   *Rabban Simeon b. Gamaliel says, "Not all courtyards are suitable for a gatehouse."*

[C]   *They force [each joint-holder to contribute to] the building of a
wall, gates, and a bolt for the town.*

[D]   *Rabban Simeon b. Gamaliel says, "Not all towns are suitable for
a wall."*

[E]   *How long must one be in a town to be deemed equivalent to all
other townsfolk?*

[F]   *Twelve months.*

[G]   *[If] one has purchased a permanent residence, lo, he is equivalent to all the other townsfolk forthwith.*

[**I**.A]   Said R. La, "[As to the reasoning of Simeon b. Gamaliel that
not all courtyards need a gate or are suitable for one,] it is normal for someone who makes a good living to build himself a
gate, [but that would not be suitable for the poor], as it is said,

'A rich man's wealth is his strong city, and like a high wall protecting him'" (Prov. 18 : 11).

[II.A] It was taught, "If one remained [in a town] thirty days, lo, he is deemed equivalent to all other townsfolk [cf. M. 1 : 4E]—as to [taking alms from, or giving to] the common fund.

[B] "As to garments, six months.

[C] "As to [being subject to] town taxes and fines, twelve months."

[D] Now is it only after all of these other things [apply to the man] that he becomes liable to town taxes and fines at the end of twelve months?

[E] Said R. Yosé b. R. Bun, "As to providing grain for the poor for the Passover, whether it is to collect food [as a poor man], or whether it is to contribute [as a rich man], [it is an obligation which applies at the end of twelve months]."

Unit I explains M. 1 : 4B, and unit II, M. 1 : 4E–F. The explanations at II B–E differ from their parallels (M.1 : 4F–G).

1 : 5   [Leiden MS and *editio princeps* 1 : 7]

[A] *They do not divide up a courtyard unless there will be [an area of] four cubits [by four cubits] for this one, and four cubits [by four cubits] for that one;*

[B] *nor [do they divide up] a field unless there will be nine qabs' space of ground for this one, and nine qabs' space for that one.*

[C] *R. Judah says, "Unless there will be nine half-qabs of space for this one, and nine half-qabs of space for that one."*

[D] *Nor [do they divide up] a vegetable patch unless there will be a half-qab of space for this one and a half-qab of space for that one.*

[E] *R. Aqiba says, "A quarter-qab's space."*

[F] *Nor [do they divide up] a banquet hall, watchtower, dovecote, cloak, bathhouse, or olive-press,*

[G]   unless there will be sufficient space for this one and sufficient space for that one.

[H]   *[Y. omits:] This is the operative principle: Whatever may be divided and [retain] its original designation do they divide.*

[I]   *But if not, they do not divide [such an object].*

[J]   *Under what circumstances? When both parties do not concur.*

[K]   *But if both parties concur,*

[L]   *even if the measurements are less than specified,*

[M]   *they divide [the area].*

[N]   *But as to Sacred Scriptures, even though both parties concur, they do not divide them.*

[I.A]   Said R. Yohanan, "The four [13a] cubits of which they have spoken [at M. 1 : 5A] are exclusive of the four cubits assigned to the doorways."

[B]   And Bar Qappara taught likewise: "They do not divide up a courtyard unless it contains eight cubits for this party, and eight cubits for that."

[C]   Said R. Yohanan, "The four cubits of which they have spoken are not necessarily such that they are permanently acquired by one of the parties, but rather a sufficient space so that he may tie up his beast for a while and undo its load."

[D]   [Objecting to this statement,] R. Jonathan raised the question: "Now did they speak of four cubits only in such wise that the man may tie up his beast for a while and undo its load? [Surely the implication of the statement that four cubits must be available is that the person must have permanent ownership of the space.]"

[E]   We find that it was taught: **Also in regard to the space around a cistern, it is assigned four cubits** [T. B.M. 11 : 15A].

[F]   The members of the house of Yannai said, "Also with regard to a chicken coop, it is assigned four cubits space round about."

[II.A]   R. Yohanan in the name of R. Benaiah: "In the case of all courtyards owned in partnership, one partner may object to what the other does in the courtyard, except for doing laundry, so as to preserve the dignity of Israelite women [that they be able to wash their garments in the courtyard and not in a public place]."

[B]   Said R. Mattenaiah, "That rule which you have stated applies solely to a place in which women do the laundry, but in a place in which men do the laundry, it is not in such [a context that the rule pertains].

[C]   "[Furthermore,] that which you have said, namely, '. . . except for doing laundry, so as to preserve the dignity of Israelite women,' [applies elsewhere in the courtyard,] but in the four cubits which belong solely to the individual, he has the right to object [to their doing laundry, and they must do it elsewhere in the courtyard].

[D]   "And as to that which you have stated, 'In the case of all court-yards owned in partnership, one partner may object to what the other does . . . ,' that applies to the entire courtyard except for the four cubits which belong to the other party, in which area the partner may not object to what the other does.

[E]   "But if the area was sloping [toward the partner's property], even in the four cubits belonging solely to the other party, the partner has every right to object [to what is done], because he has the power to claim against him, 'You pour out [slops] in your area, but it rolls down into mine.'"

[F]   R. Yohanan in the name of R. Eleazar b. R. Simeon: "He who does not want to contribute to a common symbolic meal [for joining property together for purposes of carrying about a whole, jointly owned area on the Sabbath]—they go into his house and extract a contribution to the common symbolic meal, even against his will."

[G]   For lo, it is taught, "And [if] he does not wish to contribute to the symbolic meal, [in a case in which] he does not object, they go into his house and take a contribution for the symbolic meal by force, because he does not object. But if he should object, that is not the rule."

[H]   And it has been taught along these same lines: **Partners in an alleyway may force one another to construct a side piece and cross piece for the alleyway [to constitute it a single territory for purposes of carrying about on the Sabbath]** [T. B.M. 11 : 18].

[I]   Said R. Yosé b. R. Bun, "It is not really that he does not wish to contribute to the symbolic meal. But out of pure spite, he is unwilling to contribute to the symbolic meal."

[III.A] R. Huna said, "A courtyard is divided according to its entries. [The point is that if there are three doors, the owner of two owns two-thirds of the courtyard.]"

[B]   Said R. Hisda, "The teaching applies for purposes of dividing up the manure. [But each doorway entitles the owner only to four cubits.]"

[C]   And so it was taught: [Tosefta's version] **Manure which is found in the courtyard is divided in proportion to the doorways.**

[D]   **And that which is found in a colonnade belongs to everybody** [T. B.M. 11:12].

[E]   **[Five] courtyards which make use of a single gutter, and the gutter was destroyed—**

[F]   **all of them pay for the repairs along with the first.**

[G]   **If the first repairs the part used for himself,**

[H]   **the rest pay the cost along with the second.**

[I]   **If the second repairs the part used for himself,**

[J]   **the last of them pays the cost by himself along with all of them** [T. B.M. 11:20].

[K]   **Five stories of a courtyard make use of a single gutter [house], and the gutter broke—**

[L]   **all of them pay the cost with the one at the bottom [of the gutter].**

[M]   **But the one at the bottom may pay the cost of fixing it by himself [for his own use];**

[N]   **and all the rest of them pay the cost of repairing it with the second party;**

[O]   **but the second may repair it by himself.**

[P]   **The one at the very top of all of them repairs it for his own use,**

[Q]   **but also shares in the costs of repairing it with all of the other** [T. B.M. 11:21].

[R]   If they were made to catch the rain water, they have the right to object to their use for doing laundry.

[S]   If they were made for doing laundry, they have not got the power to object to their use for collecting rain water.

[IV.A]   *But as to Sacred Scriptures, even though both parties concur, they do not divide them* [M. 1 : 5N].

[B]   Said R. Hoshaiah, "That rule applies, for example, to scrolls containing both Psalms and Chronicles. But if they are scrolls containing only Psalms, they may divide them."

[C]   Said R. Uqbah, "Even if they are scrolls containing only Psalms, they may not divide them,

[D]   "for, since they do not divide the Scroll, these parties may come and read the passages along with those, and those parties may come and read the passages along with these."

Unit **I** clarifies M. 1 : 5A, mainly supplying further data. Unit **II** proceeds to an issue only tangentially relevant to Mishnah, namely, the rights of various parties to a courtyard to prevent activities they find obnoxious. What we have at **II**.A is a general statement, extensively qualified in important ways at **II**.B–E. This discussion of mutual rights and responsibilities then moves on to the matter of yet another collective act, preparation of the symbolic meal which is deemed to unite into a single domain the several properties adjoining a given courtyard or alleyway. All parties must contribute, if the symbolic meal is to take effect and so permit the partners to carry objects about in the courtyard and so treat the courtyard as a single domain. Unit **III** returns to the matter of the division of a courtyard. Its materials again are relevant only in a general way to M. 1 : 5A. Unit **IV**, finally, brings us to M. 1 : 5N and makes an important point. We see that there is no pretense at a systematic effort to clarify Mishnah or even to develop the Talmud's own materials.

2 Yerushalmi Baba Batra
Chapter Two

2:1

[A]   *One may not dig a cistern near the cistern of his fellow,*

[B]   *nor a ditch, cave, water channel, or laundry pool,*

[C]   *unless one set it three handbreadths away from the wall of his fellow,*

[D]   *and plastered it with plaster [to retain the water].*

[E]   *They set back olive refuse, manure, salt, lime, or stones three handbreadths from the wall of one's fellow,*

[F]   *or plaster it with plaster.*

[G]   *They set back seeds, a plow, and urine three handbreadths from a wall.*

[H]   *And they set a hand mill three handbreadths from the lower millstone, which is four from the upper millstone;*

[I]   *and the oven, [so that the wall is] three handbreadths from the belly of the oven, which is four from the rim.*

[I.A]   [13b] Thus is the meaning of the Mishnah [at M. 2:1C–D], *And plastered it with plaster,* [that is to say:]

[B]   If one plastered it with plaster, [it may be set back] by any distance at all.

[C]   If he did not plaster it with plaster, [then he must set it back by three handbreadths].

[D]   [Evidence for this matter is derived] from the following: *They set back olive refuse, manure, salt, lime, or stones, three hand-*

36

breadths from the wall of one's fellow, or *plaster it with plaster*
[M. 2 : 1E–F].

[II.A]   Here you maintain that it is because rocks give out heat, and
there you maintain that they do not give out heat. [That is, one
must keep the rocks back from the wall because they give out
heat. Yet on the list of objects in which one may not keep food
warm on the Sabbath by reason of their imparting or giving out
heat, not merely preserving it, rocks are not included. Consequently, the power of rocks to give out heat is treated differently
here from M. Shab. 4 : 1ff.]

[B]   Said R. Yosé, "Here and there rocks most certainly do not give
out heat. [Then why are they listed here?] It is because rocks
near a wall make the ground around them loose and weaken the
earth of the wall [that the rule is stated here as it is, and that is
the principal consideration]."

[III.A]   It was taught: **In the case of what is a granite [not pebble]
wall, lo, it is permitted [to urinate on the wall** (T. B.B. 1 : 4D)].

[B]   Now under what circumstances do we invoke this rule? [The
following case is pertinent:]

[C]   R. Yohanan went out of the synagogue, and urinated [poured
out water] at the back of a wall.

[D]   Now we do not know whether it was because it was a granite
wall, or because he was in pain and could not keep it in.

[IV.A]   [Now as to the separation of the hand mill from the wall by three
handbreadths from the lower millstone, which is four from the
upper, as at M. 2 : H,] that rule covers the hand mill used over
there [in Babylonia].

[B]   But as to the hand mill such as we use, it must be three from the
wheel, which are four from the framework under the millstone.

[V.A]   *And the oven, so that the wall is three handbreadths from the
belly of the oven, which is four from the rim* [M. 2 : 1I].

[B]   R. Judan b. Pazzi said, "From the outer rim and inward."

[C]   And rabbis say, "From the inner rim and outward."

[D]   If it was made in the shape of a dovecote, what is the rule [as to
whether three handbreadths suffice]?

[E]   Let us derive the answer from the following:

[F]   [(Delete: R. Judah says,) *A person should not set up an oven in
a room unless there is a space of four cubits above it. If he was
setting it up in the upper story,]* there has to be a layer of plaster
under it three handbreadths thick, and in the case of a stove, a
handbreadth thick [M. 2:2A–C].

[G]   Now is not an oven shaped like a dovecote, and you then may
say, whether above or below, a handbreadth suffices?

[H]   Here too: whether above or below, three handbreadths suffice.
[We do not differentiate among the parts of the oven in the
shape of a dovecote.]

The Talmud systematically glosses and expands the Mishnah's
rules, as indicated.

2:2

[A]   *A person should not set up an oven in a room,*

[B]   *unless there is a space of four cubits above it.*

[C]   *[If] he was setting it up in the upper story, there has to be a
layer of plaster under it three handbreadths thick,*

[D]   *and in the case of a stove, a handbreadth thick.*

[E]   *And if it did damage, [the owner of the oven] has to pay for the
damage.*

[F]   *R. Simeon says, "All of these measures have been stated only so
that if [the object] inflicted damage, [the owner] is exempt from
paying compensation [if the stated measures have been
observed]."*

[I.A]   It was taught, "And not an oven belonging to a blacksmith
[unless it is given the appropriate space to avoid damage to the
neighbor's house]."

[B]   R. Qarna taught, "If it was, for example, [an oven such as
serves] a refiner or a blacksmith, it is permitted [if it was located
there] to begin with [before the other party built his house]."

[II.A]   [With reference to M. 2:2E, if it did damage, the owner has to pay, the question now is raised:] What about [damage done] to the dwelling opposite [one's oven]? [Is the owner of the oven liable to pay for damage done not in the house in which the oven is set up?]

[B]   R. Aha said, "All the more so does the rule apply to damage done by an oven to a house opposite."

[III.A]   Said R. Jonathan, "He who causes damage does not enjoy the benefit of the claim of usucaption. [That is, the claim that, since the other party suffered the damage for many years, he has reconciled himself to it. No matter when the injured party lays claim, even after years of damage, he is to be compensated.]"

[B]   R. Joshua says, "Rabbis in particular forewarn in the case of a continuing cloud of smoke [issuing from a stove]. [The one who causes the smoke cannot lay claim that the others have accepted the nuisance and need not be compensated.]"

[C]   This is in accord with the following: A woman would make a fire out of coals underneath the house of R. Ilpa. He wanted to prevent her from doing so. The case came before R. Nassah. He said, "They made the rule only in the case of a continuing cloud of smoke, [while in this case, it is only an occasional nuisance, so one may not prevent the woman from making the fire]."

Units I and II gloss Mishnah, as is clear. Unit III then raises a secondary but entirely pertinent question, on whether owners of long-term nuisances are accorded the presumption that the injured parties have accepted the situation. They are not, III A, and this is with special reference to the matter of III B, C.

2:3

[A]   *A person should not open a bakeshop or a dyer's shop under the granary of his fellow.*

[B]   *nor a cattle stall.*

[C]   *To be sure, in the case of wine they permitted doing so,*

[D]   *but not [building] a cattle stall [under the wine cellar].*

[E]   *As to a shop in the courtyard,*

[F]   *a person may object and tell [the shopkeeper], "I cannot sleep because of the noise of people coming in and the noise of people going out."*

[G]   *One may make utensils [and] go out and sell them in the market.*

[H]   *Truly one has not got the power to object and to say, "I cannot sleep because of the noise of the hammer,*

[I]   *"the noise of the millstones,*

[J]   *"or the noise of the children."*

[I.A]   R. Jacob bar Aha drove a pastry seller from one portico to another [that is, forced him to move away].

[B]   There was a pastry seller [who] opened [a store] under [the dwelling of] R. Abedomi, brother of R. Yosé. R. Aha passed by and did not object [to the opening of the store]. [R. Abedomi] said, "Rabbis pass by and do not object [to this store]!" R. Aha grew angry with him. R. Abedomi, brother of R. Yosé grew sick. He became yet sicker. R. Yosé came up to call on him. He said, "I shall go and raise the question with [Aha]." He went and spoke, and the court [on which Aha sat] gave instructions to have pity on him and to prepare burial shrouds for him [which was a sign that Aha had made his peace with the brother].

[C]   A man sold off his entire courtyard, leaving for himself one porch only. He would go up and sit there. The case came before R. Jonah b. R. Yosé. They ruled, "You do not have the right to go up and sit on the porch and watch [the owner] go in and come out of his house."

[D]   A man sold off half of his courtyard. He left for himself one bread shop [already resident in the courtyard]. The case came before R. Jonah and R. Yosé. They ruled, "You are the one who came to him. He never came to you."

[E]   And so it was taught:

[F]   **If the stall or the shop was there before the granary, [the owner of the granary] has not got the power to object [T. B.B. 1:4G].**

[II.A]   It was taught: *To be sure, in the case of wine they permitted,* even though [the heat] diminishes the wine in volume, it improves its quality.

[B]   When R. Hoshaiah heard this teaching, he put his wine onto the roof of the bathhouse. His wine soured. He said, "The Mishnah caused me to err." [Later, he stated,] "It's not that the Mishnah caused me to err. But the odor of the bathhouse soured the wine."

[III.A]   **[If the bake- or dyer's shop or cattle stall was there** before the storehouse (was built, M. 2:3A), *one has not got the power* **to stop him** and *to say, "I cannot sleep because of the noise of the hammer* **or because of the bad smell** or *because of the noise of the children"* (M. 2:3H). **As to one's neighbor in a nearby courtyard, however, one may not force him to desist from annoying practices. Rabban Simeon b. Gamaliel says, "In the case of one's neighbor, one may force him to desist from annoying practices"]** [T. B.B. 1:4]. It was taught: But [if he wanted to rent the store or the stall] to his neighbor, once he has accepted the agreement, he has not got the power to retract. [That is, once one such shop is accepted by the others in the court, they cannot object to someone else's running the same sort of shop.]

[B]   Rabban Simeon b. Gamaliel says, "Even if he has accepted the arrangement, [another resident] still has the power to retract [his acceptance of the shop].

[C]   "For he has the right to say to him, 'Those who used to come to you will come and go here asking for you when they do not find you, and they will cause much more traffic for us.'"

[D]   [As to **III.A**, If the shop was there before the storehouse,] R. Haninah and R. Mana—One said, "What is the law as to his neighbor's [retracting his agreement] when he has rented out his house to him?

[E]   "Once he has accepted the agreement, he cannot retract."

[F]   R. Huna said, "What is the law as to his neighbor's opening a store?

[G]   "Once he has accepted the agreement, he cannot retract."

[H]   This position of Rabban b. Gamaliel [B] is in accord with the view of R. Meir.

[I]   For we have learned there:

[J]   *And in the case of all of them, said R. Meir, "Even though the husband stipulated with the wife [that he has a given repulsive trait], she has the power to claim, 'I thought that I could take it, but I cannot take it'"* [M. Ket. 7:10].

[IV.A]   *Truly one has not got the power to object and to say, "I cannot sleep because of the noise of the hammer, the noise of the millstones, or the noise of the children"* [M. B.B. 2:3H–J].

[B]   These who teach children to write and reckon—their neighbors have the right to object [to their doing so in the common courtyard].

[C]   For he has the power to say to him, "They will come and go looking for you and not find you, and they will cause much more traffic for us."

[D]   These Sepphoreans objected to one another in regard to the stench of a dungheap.

[E]   R. Abimi bar Tobi gave instructions to put a dungheap [or: loom] between one wall and another wall.

[F]   R. Isaac bar Haqilah gave instruction to a lumber mill to set [the sawing] from the wall of his property at a distance of four cubits.

[G]   Said R. Yosé b. R. Bun, "These pillars which are shaky—it is from the force of the sawing that they are shaky.

[H]   "The wall of the tannery [is so shaky that] from the roar of a Persian lion it will fall down."

Unit **I** presents a set of cases illustrative of M. 2:3A–B, showing how rabbis decided conflicting claims on rights to engage in certain activities in courtyards. Unit **II** goes on to deal with M. 2:3C. Unit **III** takes up the relevant passage of Tosefta and works out the relation of that passage to M. 2:3H. There clearly are some textual problems in the arrangement of the materials of this unit, e.g., **III** C is out of place. Unit **IV** takes up the same item and presents an important qualification at **IV**.B. What C is doing here is no clearer than what it contributes earlier. D, E, F,

G–H, then give some miscellaneous illustrations of the general theme of M.

2:4

[A] *He whose wall was near the wall of his fellow*

[B] *may not build another wall next to it,*

[C] *unless he sets it four cubits back.*

[D] *[And if he builds a wall opposite his fellow's] windows, whether it is higher, lower, or opposite them,*

[E] *[he must set it back by] four cubits.*

[I.A] [With reference to M. 2:4A–C,] the members of the house of R. Yannai say, "Concerning those who come to settle in a new town does the Mishnah speak [in requiring space between one wall and another, for the constant passage of people will tred down the ground by the wall and so strengthen its foundations]. [In an old town this strengthening process already has been completed.]"

[B] [13c] Said R. La, "It is with regard to a solid wall that the Mishnah speaks."

[C] Said R. Yosé, "It is with regard to a Sodomite wall [a wall which may not have windows looking into the adjoining lot] that the Mishnah speaks [at M. 2:4A–C]."

[D] Said R. Yosé b. R. Bun, "The language of the Mishnah pericope itself indicates that that is the case [that the wall of A–C has no windows looking into the adjoining lot],

[E] "for lo, it then says, *And if he builds a wall opposite his fellow's windows, whether it is higher, lower, or opposite them, he must set it back by four cubits* [thus indicating that the earlier clause addresses a wall not opposite the fellow's window]."

[II.A] **They set a wall four cubits away from windows,**

[B] **above [and] on the sides, so that one will not see in;**

[C] **below, so that one will not peek in;**

[D] **and opposite, so that it will not cast a shadow [on the windows] [T. B.B. 1:5].**

[E]   And so it has been taught:

[F]   They set a wall at a distance from a window by the measure of the height of the window.

Unit **I** carefully explains M. 2:4A–C, and unit **II**, M. 2:4 D–E—a fine piece of close exegesis.

2:5

[A]   *They set [one's] ladder four cubits away from the dovecote [of one's neighbor],*

[B]   *so that the marten will not jump in [to the dovecote].*

[C]   *And [they set back] a wall from [one's neighbor's] roof gutter by four cubits,*

[D]   *so that [the neighbor] will be able to set up his ladder [to clean out his gutter].*

[E]   *They set up a dovecote fifty cubits away from a town.*

[F]   *And one should not set up a dovecote in his own domain, unless he has fifty cubits of space in every direction.*

[G]   *R. Judah says, "Four kors of space of ground,*

[H]   *"the length of the flight of a pigeon."*

[I]   *But if he had bought it [and it was built in that place],*

[J]   *even if it was only a quarter-qab of space,*

[K]   *lo, he retains his established right.*

[I.A]   Said R. Eleazar, "That rule which you have stated [at M. 2:5A–B], applies to a ladder at the right [of the dovecote]. But [as to a ladder set up] at the left side, one sets it up right on the spot."

[II.A]   Here you maintain that fifty cubits [is the space covered by a pigeon], while there [at M. B.Q. 7:7: *They may not set snares for pigeons unless it be thirty ris from an inhabited place]* you hold that it is a matter of thirty *ris*.

[B]   Said R. Yosé b. R. Bun, "As to the matter of feeding, a pigeon feeds in an area of fifty cubits. As to the matter of flying about, a pigeon flies about even up to four *mils*."

The Talmud's close exegesis of Mishnah continues as before.

2:6

[A]   *A fallen pigeon which is found within fifty cubits—*

[B]   *lo, it belongs to the owner of the dovecote.*

[C]   *[If it is found] outside of a fifty-cubit range,*

[D]   *lo, it belongs to the one who finds it.*

[E]   *[If] it was found between two dovecotes,*

[F]   *[if it was] nearer to this one, it belongs to him,*

[G]   *and [if it was] nearer to the other one, it belongs to him,*

[H]   *and [if it was] exactly in-between, the two of them divide it up.*

[I.A]   [As to the rule of M. 2:6E–H,] that rule which you have stated applies in a case in which the public way does not come between the two of them.

[B]   But if the public way goes between the two of them, it is not in such a case [that the rule applies]. [In this case, it need not be assigned to one or the other of the owners of the dovecotes but rather to someone who has passed by. That person despairs of recovering the pigeon and hence the one who finds it may keep it.]

[C]   We derive each rule from the other case.

[D]   [With reference to the case of finding a purse of money in an inn in which three or more are located, we assign the purse to the one who finds it, in the theory that the owner must despair of retrieving it]. [Now] we derive [that rule] from the present case [in which the public way intervenes] [cf. B.M. 2:4].

[E]   But if they were two [in the inn], then the finder must announce [what he has found and attempt to discover the true owner], [since in that case, as in the rule of Mishnah before us, there is no reason to suppose that the original owner has given up hope of finding the lost object]. [One or the other of the two owns the purse.]

[F]   And the rule pertaining to the [case of the inn, C], is derived from the present case: If they were three, the found object belongs to the one who has found it [for the owner gives up hope of recovering it].

The Talmud first inserts its own, relevant consideration into the exegesis of Mishnah, A–B, and then, on that basis, develops yet a secondary problem and its solution, as explained in square brackets. I follow PM throughout in the supplied language.

2:7–8

[A]   *They keep a tree twenty-five cubits from a town,*

[B]   *and in the case of a carob or a sycamore, fifty cubits.*

[C]   *Abba Saul says, "In the case of any sort of tree which produces no fruit, fifty cubits."*

[D]   *If the town was there first, one cuts down the tree and pays no compensation.*

[E]   *And if the tree came first, one cuts down the tree but pays compensation.*

[F]   *[If it is a matter of] doubt whether this came first or that came first,*

[G]   *one cuts down the tree and pays no compensation.*

[H]   *They set a permanent threshing-floor fifty cubits from a town.*

[I]   *A person should not build a permanent threshing-floor in his own property,*

[J]   *unless he owns fifty cubits of space in all directions.*

[K]   *And he sets it some distance away from the crops of his fellow and from his plowed land,*

[L]   *so that he will not do damage.*

[I.A]   [Is the reason that they keep trees away from towns] that it stands and casts a shadow,

[B]   or is it that it is bad for the climate?

[C]   What is the practical difference between these two proposed reasons?

[D]   It would be a case in which a tree stood within one's own property.

[E]   If you say that the reason is that it stands and casts a shadow, then a tree in one's property is permitted.

[F]   But if you say that it is because it is bad for the climate, then even a tree in one's own property is forbidden.

The Talmud takes up only M. 2:7A.

2:9

[A]   *They put carrion, graves, and tanneries at least fifty cubits away from a town.*

[B]   *They make a tannery only at the east side of a town.*

[C]   *R. Aqiba says, "In any side of it one may set it up,*

[D]   *"except for the west side.*

[E]   *"But one must in any event set it fifty cubits away [from the town]."*

[I.A]   [With reference to Aqiba's statement that one may set a tannery in any direction except on the west side of the town,] R. Abbahu in the name of R. Yohanan: "[The fifty cubits of legal distance from the inhabited place are counted from the end of the town] to the place where he flays the carcass."

[B]   Members of the household of R. Yannai say, "It is from the place at which one may stand and smell the stench of the tannery."

[C]   So too was it taught: *R. Aqiba says, "In any side of it one may set it up [namely, a tannery]* [M. 2:9C],

[D]   "and he sets it fifty cubits away,

[E]   "except for the west side,

[F]   "because [the wind] is constant" [T. B.B. 1:8].

[G]   R. Mana was traveling with people afflicted with boils. Abbaye said to him, "Do not walk at his east side but at his west side."

The Talmud complements Mishnah's rule on the tannery and cites Tosefta's version of Aqiba's saying.

2:10

[A]   They set up a pool for steeping flax away from a vegetable patch,

[B]   leeks away from onions,

[C]   and a mustard plant away from bees.

[D]   R. Yosé permits in the case of a mustard plant.

[I.A]   It was taught: They keep onions away from leeks [as well as leeks away from onions, M. 2:9B].

[B]   But R. Eleazar b. R. Simeon permits [planting onions near leeks].

[C]   Said R. Jacob b. Dosai, "[In fact, there is no disagreement between M. 2:9B and I A]. From that which is stated in the Mishnah [we derive the rule that] just as this one is kept apart from that one, so that one is kept apart from this one, [since the damage is mutual]."

[II.A]   R. Abbahu in the name of R. Yosé b. Haninah: "The reason [for M. 2:9C's rule is that] the mouth of the bees is bitter, and [when the bees come and eat honey], they will ruin the honey [through the mustard seed which they have absorbed]. [So the mustard does damage to honey.]"

The Talmud explains the reasons for Mishnah's rulings and supplies a close reading of Mishnah.

2:11–12

[A]   *They set up a tree twenty-five cubits away from a cistern,*

[B]   *and in the case of a carob and a sycamore tree, fifty cubits,*

[C]   *whether higher [than the cistern] or on the same level.*

[D]   *If the cistern was there first, one cuts down the tree and pays the value.*

[E]   *If the tree was there first, one may not cut down the tree.*

[F]   *[If it is a matter of] doubt whether this was there first or that was there first,*

[G]   *one may not cut it down.*

[H]   *R. Yosé says, "Even though the cistern was there before the tree, one may not cut down [the tree],*

[I]   *"for this one [has every right to] dig within his domain, and that one [has every right to] plant a tree within his domain."*

[J]   *A person may not plant a tree near his fellow's field,*

[K]   *unless he set it four cubits away from [the other's field].*

[L]   *All the same are vines or any other tree.*

[M]   *[If] there was a fence in-between, this one plants near the wall on the side, and that one plants near the wall on the other side.*

[N]   *[If] the roots of one's [tree] extended into the domain of the other,*

[O]   *one may cut them away down to three handbreadths,*

[P]   *so that they will not hinder the plow.*

[Q]   *[If] one was digging a cistern, ditch, or cave,*

[R]   *he may cut off the roots as far as he digs down,*

[S]   *and the wood is his.*

[I.A]   R. Jacob bar Idi in the name of R. Joshua b. Levi: "The reason behind the position of the rabbis [at M. 2:10D, that if the cistern was there first, one cuts down the tree] is that the possibility for habitation of the world depends upon cisterns."

[B]   Simeon bar Vava said in the name of R. Yohanan: "Thus did R. Yosé [M. 2:10H] reply to sages: 'Just as you maintain that the possibility for habitation of the world depends upon cisterns, so I maintain that the possibility for habitation of the world depends upon trees.'"

[**II**.A]   [With reference to M. Bik. 1:1: *So too he who sinks a shoot from a tree planted in another's domain or the public domain so that it grows in his own domain does not bring first fruits*, the reason is that the fruits do not derive wholly from land belonging to that farmer. *R. Judah says, "Such a one may bring them."* In the exposition of that matter the following discussion is presented. The full details will be laid out in that context.] Said R. Yosé, "And well did he say so.

[B]   "For if one rules that the matter of roots are the principal consideration in regard to the obligation to bringing first fruits [so that if one does not have complete ownership of the ground in which the roots are growing, he need not bring first fruits deriving from that tree], then a man will never be able to bring first fruits, for the roots of this tree extend into the roots of that one, and vice versa. [Accordingly, the principal consideration cannot be sole ownership of the entire area in which the roots are growing.]"

[C]   On that account said R. Yosa in the name of R. Yohanan: "The question of the location of the roots so far as the obligation to bring first fruits is null."

Unit **I** interprets M. 2:10D, H, and unit **II**, borrowed, as indicated, from M. Bik. 1:1, relates to M. 2:10Nff.

2:13–14

[A]   *A tree which stretches over into the field of one's fellow—*

[B]   *one cuts it away [to a height measured] as far as one reaches by an ox goad held over the plow,*

[C]   *and, in the case of a carob and a sycamore, according to the measure of the plumb line [right at the boundary].*

[D]   *In the case of an irrigated field, [he may cut away] any sort of tree by the measure of the plumb line [right at the boundary].*

[E]   *Abba Saul says, "In the case of any tree which yields no fruit, [one may cut away] by the measure of the plumb line [right at the boundary]."*

[F]   *[In the case of] a tree which extends into the public domain,*

[G]   *one cuts [the branches] so that a camel may pass with its rider.*

[H]   *R. Judah says, "[A camel] carrying flax or bundles of branches."*

[I]   *R. Simeon says, "Every tree [is to be cut away] in accord with the measure of a plumb line,*

[J]   *"because of [overshadowing a passing corpse and spreading] uncleanness."*

[I.A]   R. Jonathan was an exemplary judge. He had as a neighbor an Aramaean [pagan], who lived cheek by jowl in the field and in the village. Now R. Jonathan had a tree planted [so that it overshadowed the property] of the Aramaean. A case along the lines [of the situation prevailing for Jonathan and his Aramaean neighbor] came before [Jonathan]. He said to them, "Go and come back tomorrow." Now the Aramaean thought to himself, "It is on my account that he made no ruling. Tomorrow I shall go and chop off the branches which overshadow my property on my own, and I shall see how he decides the other case. If he judges other people but does not apply the judgment to himself, he is not a decent person." At evening R. Jonathan sent instructions to his carpenter, saying, "Go, cut off the part of the tree which is overshadowing the Aramaean's land." In the morning, the litigant came before R. Jonathan. He said to him, "Go, cut the branches which are overhanging into your land." The Aramaean then said to him, "And what is the law about your branches?" He said to him, "Go and see how my branches are treated in your property [for they already had been cut off]." He went out and saw the pruning which had taken place, and he said, "Blessed be the God of the Jews."

[B]   A certain woman [having a case before Jonathan] brought him a present of figs. He said to her, "By your leave, if you brought them in uncovered, bring them out uncovered, and if you brought them in covered up, bring them out covered up, so that people won't say that you brought in money, when you in fact brought a gift of figs [which in any case I shall not accept]."

[C]   R. Haninah came to visit R. Jonathan in his garden, and he [i.e., Jonathan] brought him figs to eat. When he went out he saw that [elsewhere in the garden] he had white Bath Sheba figs [that is, figs of a far higher quality]. He said to him, "Now why did you not feed me some of these [which are of better quality]?" He said to him, "They are my son's." R. Haninah had scruples about taking them without permission from the son and so committing an act of theft against him.

[II.A]   R. Yosa in the name of R. Yohanan, "The law is in accord with R. Simeon [at M. 211I]."

[B]   R. Hiyya in the name of R. Yohanan: "Everyone concurs that the law is in accord with R. Simeon."

The theme of chopping down branches accounts for the inclusion of I.A, and, in its aftermath, B, C.

3 Yerushalmi Baba Batra
Chapter Three

3:1

[A]   *[Title by] usucaption of houses, cisterns, trenches, caves, dovecotes, bathhouses, olive-presses, irrigated fields, slaves,*

[B]   *and anything which continually produces a yield—*

[C]   *title by usucaption applying to them is three years,*

[D]   *from day to day [that is, three full years].*

[E]   *A field which relies on rain—[title by] usucaption for it is three years,*

[F]   *not from day to day [Danby: "And they need not be completed"].*

[I.A]   [13d] How do we know that ownership through usucaption [is established through three years of unharassed occupancy]?

[B]   Said R. Yohanan, "We have heard from those who go to Usha: 'They have derived the rule from the analogy of an ox which is an attested danger [after three distinct episodes of goring]. [Likewise, once three years have passed without objection from the putative owner, the right of ownership through usucaption is established.]'"

[C]   [Objecting to this claim,] said R. Yosé, "Who holds the position that an ox is declared an attested danger only if it has gored on three distinct days? Is it not [only] R. Judah? [But R. Meir maintains that the three gorings may be on a single day, and were the analogy drawn to his view, the full period of usucaption would be a single year.]"

[D]   [Indeed, the analogy is solely to Judah's position in the present context. We shall see that it is Judah's view which prevails overall] for we have learned there: *Said R. Judah, "They specified a period of three years only so that one may be located in Ispamia, and [thus] one may hold possession for a year, [and in the second year] people will go and inform [the owner] over the period of a year, and [the owner] may return in the third year* [M. B.B. 3:3E].

[II.A]   Simeon bar Vava in the name of R. Yohanan: "He who sells a house to his fellow—once he has handed the key over to him, [the purchaser] has acquired possession of the house."

[B]   R. Ami in the name of R. Yohanan: "He who sells a house to his fellow, once [the purchaser] has stored produce in the house, he has acquired possession of it."

[C]   Said R. Samuel bar R. Isaac, "But this is on condition that the produce is of a sort which is suitable for storage."

[D]   R. Yohanan in the name of R. Yannai: "He who sells a cistern to his fellow, once he has handed over to him the bucket, [the purchaser] has acquired possession of it."

[E]   R. Joshua b. Levi in the name of R. Simeon b. Laqish: "He who sells a flock to his fellow, once he has handed over to him the leading implements, the purchaser has acquired possession of it."

[F]   What is the meaning of "leading implements"?

[G]   There are those who say it is the staff; there are those who say it is the pipe; and there are those who say it is the bellwether.

[H]   R. Simeon b. Laqish in the name of Bar Qappara: "He who sells a grave to his fellow—once the latter has buried one corpse in one of the niches, it is a mark of presumptive possession of the whole niche area.

[I]   "If he has buried three corpses in three niches, it is a mark of presumptive possession of the entire grave area."

[III.A] *And slaves* [M. 3:1A]:

[B]   R. Simon, brother of R. Judah bar Zabedi, in the name of Rab: "As to an infant, so long as it is lying in the market place, its father or mother may give testimony [as to its genealogical sta-

tus]. Once it has been taken out of the market place [as a found-
ling], it is necessary for two witnesses to give evidence as to its
genealogical status. And its father and its mother are treated as
two witnesses."

[C]   Said R. Abbahu, "And a man [the father] is suspect of stating
concerning one who is not his son that he is his son,

[D]   "lest such a statement may have been made in regard to the
property owned by a proselyte [which is deemed ownerless]. [A
man's claim that the man is his son thus can produce a material
benefit, since the man then may inherit the property of the
proselyte.]

[E]   He [Simon] said to him, "Lo, all our rabbis in the Exile give
testimony concerning us that thus have we heard from R. Ada
bar Abbahu, said R. Hisda, 'That which you have said applies to
an infant which does not crawl about [leave the place where it
was put down].'

[F]   "But in the case of an infant which can leave the place in which
it is put down, [the father and mother are not accepted as
witnesses]."

[G]   This is in line with that which R. Yohanan said, "Calves and
foals which leap about from place to place are not subject to
acquisition through usucaption."

[IV.A]   R. Yasa in the name of R. Yohanan: "Two fields which are part
of the estate of a proselyte, with a pathway between them—if
one has uprooted [weeds or branches] from one of them [intend-
ing] to acquire the other field and not to acquire the pathway—

[B]   "the field [from which he removed the weeds] is acquired, but
the other field is not."

[C]   R. Zira raised the question before R. Yasa: "If one intended to
effect acquisition of the path and that which is below it [what is
the law]?"

[D]   Said R. Hisda, "As to the estate of a proselyte, if one has
gathered weeds at the northern part of a field intending to acquire the southern part of the field but not the part in the middle—the northern part of the field he has acquired, the southern
part he has not acquired."

[E]   There we have learned: *[He who purchases flax from his fellow—lo, this one has not acquired possession until he will move it from one place to another. But] if it was attached to the ground and he has plucked any small quantity of it, he has acquired possession* [M. B.B. 5:7].

[F]   Samuel said, "He has acquired only what he has plucked up."

[G]   Said R. Abedoma, the emigrant, "This statement [of Samuel's] was made with reference to the estate of a proselyte [as at **IV.A–B**]."

[H]   R. Hisda, said R. Isaac, "Because you do not wish to say that this [M. B.B. 5:7] poses a problem to Samuel, you state that the rule treats a case involving the estate of a proselyte."

[I]   R. Hisda said, "If one has drawn this beast intending to acquire it, he has acquired it. If he did so in order to acquire its offspring, he has acquired them. If he did so in order to acquire it and its offspring, he has not effected acquisition."

[J]   Said R. Nissah, "That rule which you have stated applies to a case in which it was not pregnant. But if it was pregnant, they have treated the fetus as equivalent to one of its limbs [and it is acquired]."

[K]   And has it not been taught:

[L]   He who sells the fetus in his beast to his fellow has done nothing at all [contrary to J]?

[M]   If he sold the fetus of his maidservant to his fellow, he has done nothing at all.

[N]   If he sold the tithes of his field to his fellow, he has done nothing whatsoever.

[O]   If he sold the air space of his ruined house to his fellow, he has done nothing whatsoever.

[P]   But he sells him his beast and leaves the fetus for himself.

[Q]   He sells him the maidservant and leaves the fetus for himself.

[R]   He sells him his field and leaves the tithes for himself.

[S]   He sells him his ruined house and leaves the air space for himself.

[V.A]   R. Ba in the name of R. Hisda, "There are three who are believed if they give testimony forthwith [upon the matter about
which they testify]: A midwife, a caravan [which finds a found-
ling], and she who declares her fellow women to be clean [by
taking responsibility for a drop of blood]."

[B]   The midwife—when she is yet seated at the travailing stool.

[C]   This is in line with the following verse of Scripture: "And the
midwife took and bound [14a] on his hand a scarlet thread, saying, 'This came out first'" (Gen. 38:28).

[D]   A caravan—

[E]   This is in accord with that which was stated by R. Simon,
brother of R. Judah bar Zabedi in the name of Rab: "As to an
infant, so long as it is lying in the market place, its father or
mother may give testimony as to its genealogical status. Once it
has been taken out of the market place [as a foundling], it is
necessary for two witnesses to give evidence as to its genealogical
status. And its father and mother are treated as two witnesses."
[Above III.B.]

[F]   A woman who gives testimony that her fellow women are
clean—

[G]   This is in line with that which we have learned there: *Three
women who were sleeping in one bed, and blood was found under one of them—all of them are unclean. [If] one of them examined herself and found herself unclean, she alone is unclean,
and the two others are clean* (M. Nid. 9:4).

[H]   Said R. Ba, "And this is on condition that it is within a period of
twenty-four hours [from the discovery of the original menstrual
blood]."

Ownership is proved not only by documentary evidence, but
also by testimony that a person has held, and enjoyed the usufruct of, a property for a given period of time. One may lose his
deed and retain the land. The present chapter expounds the
rules of acquiring or securing title through usucaption, specifying the conditions under which such a claim may be made and
effected, the sorts of things subject to that particular process

for establishing ownership, and related questions of squatters' rights. The basic rule at M. 3:1 is somewhat complicated, because there are some secondary issues inserted into the primary declaration of A, C. The first is the consideration at B, and the second, D/F. Anything which is valuable and is allowed to remain in the hands of a person for a period of three years is assumed to belong to that person. If there were a valid claim against the squatter, any other party would have made it within the specified time. The Talmud's treatment of the Mishnah rule is curiously halting. The opening unit identifies the reasoning behind the principal detail of Mishnah, the notion that usucaption is effected in a three year period. This is the sole exegesis of Mishnah. Unit **II** simply presents a repertoire of other modes of acquisition and when they take effect—not one of them pertinent to what is before us in any way. Unit **III** deals with testimony as to the status of individuals; it has no direct reference to the lemma of Mishnah cited at **III.**A. Unit **IV** reverts to the matter of effecting acquisition, but not through usucaption such as Mishnah knows. Unit **V** runs over the materials of unit **III**. How all of this advances the interpretation of Mishnah or of the rules relevant to Mishnah is not at all clear.

3:2

[A]   R. Ishmael says, "Three months in the first year, three in the last, and twelve months in between—lo, eighteen months [suffices to fill out the three years]."

[B]   R. Aqiba says, "A month in the first year, a month in the last, and twelve months in between—lo, fourteen months."

[C]   Said R. Ishmael, "Under what circumstances?

[D]   "In the case of a sown field.

[E]   "But in the case of a tree-planted field, [if] one has brought in the [grape crop], collected the olives, and gathered the [fig] harvest,

[F]   "lo, these [three harvests] count as three years."

[I.A]   Samuel said, "This represents the view of R. Ishmael and R. Aqiba.

[B] "But sages say, '[Ownership through usucaption is established only through] three years of harvesting the grain, three years of vintaging the grapes, three years of cutting the olives.'"

[C] Rab said, "This represents the view of R. Ishmael and R. Aqiba.

[D] "But sages say, '[Ownership through usucaption is established only through] three full years ['from day to day'].'"

[E] R. Samuel bar Nahman in the name of R. Jonathan: "Just as they differ here, so they differ with regard to the three years referred to by Elijah [in which there will not be dew or rain]. [At issue is whether three complete years or three seasons is meant.]"

[F] [Leiden lacks this stich; It is misplaced in *editio princeps* after 3:3IA:] Said R. Hanina, "The years counted for the prohibition of the produce of an orchard in the first three years of its planting is the practical difference between the opinions expressed here. [That is, do we count three full years, as sages would say, or three harvest-seasons, which may be considerably less than three full years?]"

The Talmud's clarification of M. is clear and disciplined.

3:3

[A] *There are three regions so far as securing title through usucaption [is concerned]: Judah, TransJordan, and Galilee.*

[B] *[If] one was located in Judea, and [someone else] took possession of his property in Galilee,*

[C] *[or] was in Galilee, and someone took possession [of his property] in Judea,*

[D] *it is not an effective act of securing title through usucaption—*

[E] *until [the owner] is with [the squatter] in the same province.*

[F] *Said R. Judah, "They specified a period of three years only so that one may be located in Ispamia, and [the squatter] may hold possession for a year; [in the second year] people will go and inform [the owner] over the period of a year, and [in the third year] he may return over the period of another year."*

[I.A]   Rab said, "[The rule that usucaption is effective only if the owner is in the same province with the squatter] was taught only with reference to times of upheaval [in which transportation is interrupted]."

[B]   Rab said, "Acquisition of property through usucaption does not apply in the case of a [landowner] who fled [his property], nor does the mode of usucaption apply from one country to another [that is, when the owner is in a different country from his land]."

[C]   Samuel said, "Acquisition of property through usucaption does apply in the case of a [landowner] who fled [his property], and it does apply from one country to another [as explained at B]."

[D]   Said R. Nahman bar R. Isaac, "Scripture supports that which Samuel has said, 'So the king appointed an official for her, saying, Restore all that was hers, together with all the produce of the fields from the day that she left the land until now' (2 Kings 8:6). [She had fled to the land of the Philistines, and her property had been seized by squatters during that time. Since the king had to restore the property, it indicates that usucaption may be effected of the property of one who has fled.]"

[E]   [With reference to the inapplicability of usucaption in a case in which the owner is in another province, M. 3:3E,] said R. Eleazar, "And even in the case of two hyparchies, for instance, Shelumi and Nabiro, with the Jordan between them, and with the owner standing there and able to see someone taking possession of his field and taking possession of his property—the squatter does not effect ownership through usucaption until the original owner is with him in that same city or province."

[II.A]   Rab said, "The principal action effecting usucaption is harvesting the produce. [That is, the testimony of the witnesses must be that they have seen the squatter harvest the produce of the field.]"

[B]   And does not Rab concur that if one weeds and hoes [the field, that too constitutes an act of usucaption]?

[C] Rab certainly does concede that if one weeds and hoes the field, [it does constitute an act of usucaption].

[D] What then is the meaning of Rab's statement, "The principal action effecting usucaption is harvesting the produce"?

[E] It is that if witnesses have seen the squatter plowing, reaping, making sheaves, threshing, sifting, but did not see him bring the produce in, that does not constitute a valid statement of evidence of usucaption. The only such valid evidence constitutes bringing in the produce.

[F] Rab said, "The principal action involved in the rite of removing the shoe [of the brother-in-law who declines to marry his childless brother's widow] is the loosing of the straps [of the sandal]."

[G] Now did not R. Ba in the name of R. Judah, state, [and also] R. Zeriqan presented the same teaching in the name of Rab: "In the opinion of sages, if the Levirate sister-in-law removed the shoe but did not spit, spit but did not remove the shoe, her rite of removing the shoe is not valid—until she will both remove the shoe and also spit"? [Consequently, the aforecited statement contradicts the present view that the principal action is not alone in removing the shoe.]"

[H] Rab certainly does concede that [the rite is not valid] until one has both removed the shoe and spit.

[I] What then is the meaning of Rab's statement, "The principal action involved in the rite of removing the shoe is the loosing of the straps of the sandal"? [In this text the question is not answered.]

[III.A] R. Yosé b. Haninah asked R. Yohanan, "[If the owner of a property] enters a complaint [against the squatter], what is the law as to his having to do so before a court?"

[B] R. Yosé in the name of R. Yohanan: "[If] one raises a complaint, he does not have to do so before a court."

[C] There are those who teach [the aforestated matter as follows:]

[D] R. Yosé b. R. Haninah asked the disciples of R. Yohanan, "[If the owner of a property] raises a complaint [against the squatter], what is the law as to his having to do so before a court?"

[E]   R. Hiyya in the name of R. Yohanan: "[If] one raises a complaint, he must do so before a court."

[F]   Samuel said, "Even if one has raised a complaint with [the squatter] before the workers, that constitutes a valid act of complaint."

[G]   And does one have to enter a complaint for each of the three years [at the outset, or, if the property is held over a long period of years, must the complaint be entered annually even after the first three years' complaints]?

[H]   Gidul bar Minyamin had a case [in which he had entered a complaint for the first three years only]. The judges of his case were Hilqiah bar Tobi, R. Huna, and Hiyya bar Rab. Hiyya bar Rab said to them, "Thus did father say: 'Once he has entered a complaint against [the squatter] for the first three years, he does not again have to enter a complaint against him.'"

[I]   And so it has been taught:

[J]   **[If] one enjoyed the usufruct of a field for six years,**

[K]   **and [the other party] complained against him for the first three years [of his usucaption]—**

[L]   **and at the end, the holder of the field said to him, "But you yourself sold it to me," "You yourself gave it to me as a gift"** [M. 3:4F]—this does not effect ownership through usucaption.

[M]   [If it is] **by reason of his original complaint, he has not secured title through usucaption** [T. B.B. 2:4].

[N]   For any act of usucaption which is not accompanied by a claim of legitimate ownership, is no act of usucaption.

[O]   Samuel said, "If this is [how the law is to be established], we are not going to leave the possibility of growing produce in the Land of Israel [since squatters will have no chance to improve the land, but will lose out even after many years]."

Unit **I** presents a systematic clarification of the matter of the location of the owner of a property in a province distant from the property subject to a squatter's claim. Unit **II** goes on to the matter of what a squatter does to effect ownership through usucaption. The position of Rab is what is clarified, and this drags

in its wake a construction formally parallel in all ways. Unit **III**
then takes up the sort of complaint the owner must enter against
the squatter, specifically, whether this must be before a court.
The text of Tosefta at **III**.J–N is somewhat confused, but the
main point is clear. The Talmud thus takes up the principal
points of Mishnah systematically and thoroughly.

3:4

[A] *Any act of usucaption [along] with which [there] is no claim [on
the property being utilized] is no act of securing title through
usucaption.*

[B] *How so?*

[C] *[If] he said to him, "What are you doing on my property?"*

[D] *and the other party answered him, "But no one ever said a thing
to me!"—*

[E] *this is not usucaption.*

[F] *[If he answered,] "For you sold it to me," "You gave it to me as
a gift," "Your father sold it to me," "Your father gave it to me
as a gift"—*

[G] *lo, this is [a valid claim of] usucaption.*

[H] *He who holds possession because of an inheritance [from the
previous owner] requires no further [legitimating] claim [in his
own behalf].*

[I.A] [But he who holds possession because of an inheritance, while
requiring no further legitimating claim in his own behalf,] does
have to effect usucaption [through utilizing the property for a
period of three years].

[II.A] [At M. Ket. 1:6–8, Joshua takes the position that the defendant must bring proof for her claim. For example, if a woman
claimed to have lost the tokens of virginity through an accident,
and the husband said she had had sexual relations with someone,
Gamaliel and Eliezer accept the woman's claim, while Joshua
states, "We do not rely on her word. She must be presumed to
have suffered intercourse before betrothal unless she can bring
proof for her claim." At M. Ket. 2:2, in this same context, we

find the following, cited only in part in our text:] There we are taught: *But R. Joshua concedes that if a person said to his fellow, "This field [belonged to your father and I bought it from him," he may be believed, for the mouth that prohibited is the mouth that permitted].* [The man volunteered the information that the claimant's father did own the property, but then claims that he had purchased it. If we accept the former claim, we accept the latter. In elucidation of M. B.B. 3:4F's claim and the matter of inheritance, M. B.B. 3:4H, this discussion now unfolds.]

[B]   Here is [an illustration of the matter]. Reuben enjoys the usufruct of a field, in the assumption that it belongs to him. Simeon produces witnesses that his father died while in possession of the field. They remove the field from the possession of Reuben and hand it over to Simeon.

[C]   But if Reuben went and brought witnesses that [Simeon's] father had not died while in possession of the field [then the claim of Simeon is null].

[D]   Said R. Nahman bar Jacob, "I am the one who took it away from Reuben. I am the one who will return it to him."

[E]   [Disagreeing with this view that the court must act afresh,] Rab said, "When you handed it over, you handed it over at the instruction of a court. From that time on, he who wishes to exact property from his fellow must bring evidence in behalf of his claim [and it is therefore Reuben's task to prove that he owns the field, for the deed of the court is effective until Reuben proves otherwise]."

[F]   But who indicates [who is the one who has to bring proof, since each party now has two valid witnesses to his claim]?

[G]   Said R. Ba, "Witnesses to the situation prevailing at the time of death indicate [which party is in presumptive possession of the property]. [Simeon has to find witnesses to indicate that his father had owned the field at the time of his death.]"

[H]   But [should you not] take note of the case in which there are no witnesses who are informed [of the situation prevailing at the time of death]?

[I]   Said R. Yosé, "The field under all circumstances remains in the presumptive possession of its owner. Henceforward, he who wishes to exact property from his fellow must bring evidence in behalf of his claim."

The Talmud clarifies M. 3:4H and, on account of the matter of inheritance, proceeds to a case parallel to, but not directly relevant, to Mishnah's rule. The issue now is not effecting possession through usucaption but indicating the claimant who bears the burden of proof. So the pericope is more naturally located at Y. Ket. 2:2 than here.

3:5

[A]   *[Craftsmen,] partners, sharecroppers, and trustees are not able to secure title through usucaption.*

[B]   *A husband has no claim of usucaption in his wife's property,*

[C]   *nor does a wife have a claim of usucaption in her husband's property,*

[D]   *nor a father in his son's property,*

[E]   *nor a son in his father's property.*

[F]   *Under what circumstances?*

[G]   *In the case of one who effects possession through usucaption [against a claim of theft].*

[H]   *But in [the case of] one who gives a gift,*

[I]   *or of brothers who divide an estate,*

[J]   *or of one who seizes the property of a proselyte,*

[K]   *[if] one has locked up [a beast], walled in [a field], or broken down [a wall] in any measure at all,*

[L]   *lo, this constitutes securing a claim through usucaption.*

[I.A]   *Partners* [M. 3:5A]:

[B]   Samuel said, "'A partner' does not belong here [on Mishnah's list]."

[C]   Does not a partner effect title through usucaption?

[D] Did not Samuel say, "A partner who goes down [into a field] and sows [a crop] is as one who sows a crop with the owner's permission [so he is not in the status of one who can effect possession through usucaption]."

[E] That which you say, that a partner who went down and sowed a crop is in the status of one who sows with permission, pertains to a case in which the partner is standing there.

[F] And that which you say, that the partner does have a claim of usucaption, pertains to a case in which the other partner is not standing there.

[G] What does [Samuel] introduce [into the Mishnah] in place of [the partner]?

[H] *Craftsmen* and thieves are not able to secure title through usucaption.

[I] [The following is an example: (Tosefta's version)] **Craftsmen are not able to effect title through usucaption. How so?] [If] one saw his utensils at a laundryman's shop,**

[J] **or his slave at a craftsman's shop,**

[K] **[If the laundryman or the craftsman] said to him, "You sold them to me," or, "You gave them to me as a gift,"**

[L] **it is not a valid claim of title through usucaption** [craftsmen are not able to secure title merely by having use of an object, since it is assumed that utensils are left with them for the owner's benefit, and the owner need not protest in order to retain his rights of ownership.]

[M] **[If he said,] "You told me to sell them," or, "You told me to give them away as a gift,"**

[N] **lo, this constitutes a valid claim of effecting title through usucaption** [T. B.B. 2:6].

[II.A] *Sharecroppers* [M. 3:5A]:

[B] R. Huna said, "[That statement] applies to a sharecropper with a permanent arrangement [who cannot establish a claim of ownership through usucaption].

[C] "But as to a sharecropper for a limited period, he can establish a claim of ownership through usucaption."

[D]   Both R. Yohanan and R. Simeon b. Laqish say, "Even a share-cropper for a limited period cannot establish claim of ownership through usucaption."

[E]   "For [the owner] of the field may claim, 'I had satisfaction [from his tenancy], so I left him on the field [for many years].'"

[F]   There [in Babylonia] they say, "A sharecropper cannot establish a claim of ownership through usucaption.

[G]   "The son of a sharecropper can establish a claim of ownership through usucaption."

[H]   Both R. Yohanan and R. Simeon b. Laqish say, "Neither a sharecropper nor the son of a sharecropper can establish a claim of ownership through usucaption.

[I]   "For the owner of the field may say, 'I had satisfaction from his father's tenancy, so I left his son on the land.'"

[J]   For R. Yohanan said, "A sharecropper who put another share-cropper on the land—the latter cannot establish a claim of own-ership through usucaption.

[K]   "For it is routine for a sharecropper to introduce another share-cropper to tend the land."

[**III.A**]   Truly: a man who oversees the property of his wife has the power to establish the claim of ownership through usucaption, for it is routine for husbands to oversee the possessions of their wives.

[B]   *A husband has no claim of usucaption in his wife's property* [M. 3:5B].

[C]   That rule applies during the lifetime of his wife. But after her death, he has a claim of usucaption in his wife's property.

[D]   *Nor does a wife have a claim of usucaption in her husband's property* [M. 3:5C].

[E]   That is true during his lifetime. But after death, she does have such a claim.

[F]   *Nor does a father have a claim of usucaption in his son's prop-erty* [M. 3:5D].

[G]   That is true during his lifetime. But after his death, he does have such a claim.

[H]   *Nor does a son in his father's property* [M. 3:5E].

[I]   That is true during his lifetime. But after his death, he does have such a claim.

[IV.A]   *[If one has locked up a beast, walled in a field, or broken down a wall, in any measure at all, lo, this constitutes securing a claim through usucaption* (M. 3:5K–L).]* Rab said, "That applies when one fills in a break in the wall to less than ten handbreadths in breadth, or adds to it so that it is ten handbreadths in height [and so completes the wall]."

[B]   Samuel said, "Even if one has broken down a place which is not suitable for an opening, or walled in a place which is not suitable for shutting up, lo, this establishes the right of ownership through usucaption."

[C]   For has it not been taught: He who sells something to his fellow, and the purchaser tarries and does not take possession of the object,

[D]   if then the seller goes and takes possession of the object,

[E]   does the act of taking possession nullify the sale or the gift?

Once more we have a systematic amplification of Mishnah's rules. Unit **I** takes up Samuel's view that Mishnah should omit reference to partners and include craftsmen. This latter item then is amply illustrated through Tosefta. Unit **II** proceeds to the next item, sharecroppers, and the course of the discussion adequately spells out what concerns the Talmud. Unit **III** systematically cites and glosses Mishnah, as indicated, and unit **IV** clarifies a minor detail.

3:6

[A]   *[If] two were testifying of another party that he has enjoyed the usufruct of the property for three years,*

[B]   *and they turn out to be false witnesses,*

[C]   *they must pay to [the original owner] full restitution (Deut. 19:19).*

[D]   [If] two witnesses [testify] concerning the first year, two concerning the second, and two concerning the third—

[E]   they divide up [the costs of restitution] among themselves.

[F]   Three brothers, and another party joins together with [each of] them—

[G]   lo, these constitute three distinct acts of testimony,

[H]   and they count as a single act of witness [when the evidence is proved false].

[I.A]   [The former owner] said to him, "What are you doing in my property?"

[B]   [The other replied,] "I have a claim for the field established through [three] years of usucaption."

[C]   And [the squatter] went and brought witnesses that he indeed had a claim on the field for the requisite years of usucaption.

[D]   Then the [other party] went and secured the proof of perjury for the witnesses [brought by the squatter]—

[E]   lo, this one [the squatter] gives him back the field and value of the produce that he had consumed over a period of three years [and this explains the compensation required at M. 3:6C].

[II.A]   [The following statement is relevant to M. B.Q. 7:3 and should not be cited here at all:] Said R. Zira, "That is to say, A perjured witness is not invalidated in court." [This matter will be dealt with *ad loc.*]

Unit **I** spells out at E the meaning of the full restitution called for by Mishnah. The purpose of M. 3:6A–C is to introduce D–E, F–H. Several pairs of witnesses join together to prove usucaption. Three brothers, each testifying about one year, join with a second party for each year to constitute valid testimony. If they are proved false, H, the outsider pays half, and each brother a sixth, of the costs of restitution.

3:7

[A]   *What are [usages] which are effective in the securing of title
through usucaption, and what are [usages] which are not effective in the securing of title through usucaption?*

[B]   *[If] one put cattle in a courtyard, put an oven, double-stove,
millstone, raised chickens, or put his manure, in a courtyard—*

[C]   *this is not an effective mode of securing title through
usucaption.*

[D]   *But [if] he made a partition for his beast ten handbreadths high,*

[E]   *and so too for an oven; so too for a double stove; so too for a
millstone—*

[F]   *[if] he brought his chickens into the house,*

[G]   *or made a place for his manure three handbreadths deep or three
handbreadths high—*

[H]   *lo, this is an effective mode of securing title through usucaption.*

[I.A]   Said R. Eleazar, "Partners are accustomed to permit one another
[to do as they like] with chickens."

[B]   Said R. Yosé, "The Mishnah has not taken [14b] that position.
But: *If two partners made a vow not to benefit from one another
. . . each is forbidden to put [in the courtyard] a millstone or an
oven or to rear chickens*" [M. Ned. 5:1]. [This item is truncated
and fully clear only at M. Ned. 5:1.]

[II.A]   Said R. Eleazar, "Tending chickens in a courtyard which does
not belong to one—lo, this is a means of securing ownership
through usucaption."

[B]   Said R. Yosé, "And that is fair enough. What is your choice? If
he has a right to raise his chickens there, lo, this one has done
so. And if he does *not* have the right to raise his chickens there
[but has done so anyhow], lo, this is a valid means of securing
ownership through usucaption."

The Talmud lightly amplifies Mishnah's rule.

3:8

[A]   *A gutterspout does not [impart title through] usucaption [so that the spout still may be moved], but the place on which it discharges does impart title through usucaption [so that the place must be left for its present purpose].*

[B]   *A gutter does [impart title through] usucaption.*

[C]   *An Egyptian ladder does not [impart title through] usucaption, but a Tyrian ladder does [impart title through] usucaption.*

[D]   *An Egyptian window does not [impart title through] usucaption, but a Tyrian window does [impart title through] usucaption.*

[E]   *What is an Egyptian window? Any through which the head of a human being cannot squeeze.*

[F]   *R. Judah says, "If it has a frame, even though a human being's head cannot squeeze through, lo, it does [impart title through] usucaption."*

[I.A]   R. Simeon b. Laqish said, "[*A gutterspout does not impart title through usucaption so that the spout still may be moved*], so far as lengthening or broadening it. [The owner of the courtyard can prevent the owner of the gutterspout from broadening or lengthening the spout, which would take up more space than the spout presently uses.]"

[B]   R. Yohanan said, "[There is no title] for that entire direction [one particular end of the gutter] [so that the owner of the courtyard may shift the direction in which the spout pours out its water, and the owner of the waterspout cannot insist that the spout must pour out the waters only in its original direction]. [But the owner of the courtyard cannot wholly remove the waterspout.]"

[C]   For have we not learned: The place on which the gutterspout debouches has a permitted domain of four cubits [into which it may routinely discharge]?

[D]   Now can you claim that that domain is limited to a single direction [end of the gutter]? [Obviously not!]

[E]   [Referring once more to Yohanan's statement,] *A gutterspout does not impart title through usucaption*—in that entire direction [since it does not matter to the owner of the spout in which direction the spout debouches].

[F]   And so has it been taught: [Tosefta's version] **The place of the gutterspout in the courtyard is not subject to a claim of ownership through usucaption. The place onto which the gutterspout discharges is subject to a claim of ownership through usucaption** [T. B.B. 2:13].

[II.A]   [As to the Egyptian ladder,] the members of the House of R. Yannai said, "A ladder of three or less rundles is considered a stool [not a ladder]."

[B]   Said R. La in the name of the members of the House of R. Yannai, "This statement was made in regard to the issue of uncleanness [that is, up to three rundles, it is deemed a stool and receives uncleanness as does any other stool]."

[C]   R. Hezekiah in the name of members of the house of R. Yannai, "It was for the matter of effecting possession through usucaption that this statement was made [thus defining the ladder for the purpose of M. 3:8C]."

[D]   R. Yosé in the name of the members of the House of R. Yannai: "It was for the matter of the Sabbath that this statement was made. [That is, a ladder serves to diminish the statutory height of a wall between two courtyards, so that, if the wall is deemed less than ten handbreadths, it is not a partition, and it may be reversed. Accordingly, if it is of the requisite height, it will serve to diminish the height of the wall, but if it is less than that height, it is not deemed a ladder at all.]"

[III.A]   [The concluding passage is relevant to M. 3:8D. What follows depends upon Y. Yeb. 12:3, as follows: What is the law as to breaking open an Egyptian window into a courtyard belonging to partners, at a height of more than four cubits? He said to him, "Do we thus rule, that the other party has the right to shut off fresh air from his nostrils?" (Obviously not!) Surely the man has a right to open what amounts to an air hole, without the other party's being able to prohibit him from doing so.] [In this matter,] said R. Hoshaiah, "They have stated this rule [that one may open an air hole at a height above four cubits from the ground] only with reference to a courtyard. But as to roofs, even a hole higher than four cubits off the ground [the other partners to the courtyard must approve, and they have a right to] prevent [one's making such a hole]."

[B]   R. Oshaiah heard this ruling, and he was displeased. He said, "I have stated a tradition, and it was not reported in my name! [So did I state matters, just as above:] 'They have stated this rule only with reference to a courtyard, but as to roofs, even a hole higher than four cubits off the ground [the other partners to the courtyard must approve, and they have a right to] prevent [one's making such a hole].'"

Unit **I** provides amplification of M. 3:8A, unit **II** takes up the Egyptian ladder, and unit **III**, the Egyptian window. That the intent is to gather available materials for the present purpose, rather than systematically to provide an exegesis of M. 3:8 in particular, is shown at unit **III**, which simply cites a few sentences, utterly out of context, because they treat the same topic as Mishnah. This is a good example of how Yerushalmi may be constructed essentially along the lines of an anthology on stated themes—artificial and jerry-built at best.

3:9

[A]   *A projection, [if it extends] a handbreadth [or more] does [impart title through] usucaption,*

[B]   *and one has the power to protest [its being made].*

[C]   *[If it projects] less than a handbreadth, it is not subject to [imparting title through] usucaption,*

[D]   *and one has not got the power to protest [its being made].*

[I.A]   R. La in the name of R. Yannai, "A projection which extends outward by a handbreadth—one may widen it as much as he wants along the length of the projection."

[B]   As to broadening it—how much [may one do so]?

[C]   Nathan son of R. Hoshaiah: "Sufficient to divide his house
       [from his neighbor's (cf. PM)]."

The Talmud amplifies Mishnah's rule.

3:10–11

[A]   *A person may not open his windows into the courtyard of which*
       he is one of the joint holders.

[B]   *[If] he purchased a house in another courtyard [which adjoins*
       the one in which he is living],

[C]   *he may not make an opening into the courtyard of which he is*
       one of the joint holders.

[D]   *[If] he built an upper story on his house, he may not make an*
       opening for it into a courtyard of which he is one of the joint
       holders.

[E]   *But if he wanted, he may build a [new] room inside of his*
       house,

[F]   *or he may build an upper story on top of his house,*

[G]   *and he may make an opening for it into his house.*

[H]   *One should not open up in a courtyard of which he is one of the*
       joint holders a doorway opposite the doorway [of another
       resident],

[I]   *or a window opposite [another's] window.*

[J]   *[If] it was small, he should not enlarge it.*

[K]   *[If it was] a single one, he should not make it into two.*

[L]   *But he may open into the public domain a doorway opposite*
       [another's] doorway [in the public domain],

[M]   *or a window opposite [another's] window [in the public*
       domain].

[N]   *If it was small, he may enlarge it.*

[O]   *If it was a single one, he may make it into two.*

[I.A]   [The inquiry is into the status of an alleyway, and the mode of inquiry is to seek implications in Mishnah's language pertinent to that intermediate space, between the outside and the inner courtyard. At issue are M. 3:10C and M. 3:10L, the former concerning the courtyard, the latter, the outside world.] Here you say that [opening] a door opposite a door is permitted [namely, at M. 3:10L], and there you say that [opening] a door opposite a doorway is prohibited [namely, at M. 3:10C].

[B]   *[Now the implication of] that which you have said [in the former instance is that it is] permitted to do so in an alleyway, and [the implication of] that which you have said [in the latter instance is that it is] forbidden to do so in an alleyway. [In the setting of the courtyard, it is forbidden to open up a new doorway; hence in an alleyway it is permitted to do so. In the setting of the outer street, it is permitted to open up a new doorway; hence in an alleyway it is prohibited to do so.]*

[C]   Now has it not been taught: **Just as joint residents of a courtyard have the power to object [to what happens in] the courtyard, so residents of a common alleyway have the power to object [to what] one another may do in the alleyway shared among them** [T. B.B. 2:15D–E].

[D]   Said R. La, "Here [in the passage in which the implication is that it is permitted to open a doorway into an alley] it is when the party living opposite has assented, and there [in the passage in which the implication that it is forbidden to do so] it is when the party living opposite has not assented [to one's opening a new doorway opposite his]."

[II.A]   [What follows takes up the passage of T. 2:15F–O, immediately following the Tosefta passage cited at I.C. The passage under discussion is as follows: **[If] one has built a bathhouse next to the bathhouse of his fellow, or a store next to the store of his fellow—[the owner of the bathhouse or store next door] cannot prevent him [from doing so], saying to him, "You have brought ruin on me." For the former may say to him, "Just as you do on your property, so I have every right to do on mine." [If] one's rainwater was pouring off into the garden of his fellow, and the latter went and stopped it up, one has the right to prevent him from doing so, unless he lets him know in which direction he is going to lead it down.** Now we notice that the rule for the bathhouse, or store, is different from the rule covering rainwater pouring off into the garden of his fellow. One cannot go and stop up the flow, and the difference between the right of the neighbor in the former instance and the one in the present instance has now to be explained.] R. Yohanan said, "The rule applying to the garden is different [from the one applying to the bathhouse or store, in which case one may not start a new bathhouse or store], because [the garden] is an area permitted for [this sort of] rutting. [So both parties are equally permitted to do the one deed but not the other.]"

[B]   Said R. Nissa, "And ruins are not allowed to be rebuilt. [That is, one cannot rebuild a fallen house in his courtyard and open up a doorway opposite an existing doorway. Along the lines of the cited passage, the other party may say that he too will want to build up a ruined house, but if the one party does so now, then the other party will be unable to open up a door later on. Consequently, both parties have the power to prohibit one another's deeds equally, just as Tosefta says.]"

[III.A]   Said R. Jacob, bar Aha, "It was taught over there [in Babylonia]: 'He who opens up a window in a wall of his courtyard in the presence of his fellow does so to a space of four cubits, opening up the wall with his left hand and sealing the hole with the right.' [That is, he must seal it immediately, since the fellow objects.]"

[B]   Now note what you have said, that if the fellow was present— [which must mean that the fellow said nothing and did not object]!

[C]   [No, that is not the meaning. The neighbor] has the power to claim, "I wanted [to see you] working hard [and troubling yourself for nought, for you were going to have to seal it up anyhow]."

[D]   [If] the neighbor even handed him the stone [for the work, so assisting him], [the neighbor still can claim that he never approved the opening of the window]. [He has] the power to claim, "I was ridiculing you [and playing a joke, since I knew you'd have to close the window up anyhow.]"

[IV.A]   **Five doors, one inside the other—the measure [to indicate whether or not uncleanness may flow through the hole] is the size of a drill. [Cf. T. Ah. 14:1C. Note T. Ah. 14:1A: A door which one made for light—its measure is the size of a drill.]**

[B]   This statement supports the position of those who say, "Those who build a window open to the *'istyb*—[such a window] is made only to bring in light."

[C]   Since it has no permanent claim [to be left where it is], it does not serve to introduce uncleanness [to the house, if a corpse should be lying under the outside roof near the window].

Unit **I** investigates a case relevant to, but not explicitly addressed by, Mishnah's law, as is spelled out. Unit **II** then takes up the exegesis of part of a passage of Tosefta introduced (but not cited in the printed text) for the work of unit **I**. Unit **III** is pertinent to Mishnah, since it gives us a picture of how one might object to a neighbor's invading his rights. Unit **IV** takes up yet another passage of Tosefta, which is explained. In all, units **I** and **III** appear to be closely linked to Mishnah, and the other two units simply pursue their own interests.

3:12

[A]   *They do not hollow out a hole under the public domain—*

[B]   *cisterns, ditches, or caves,*

[C]   *R. Eliezer permits,*

[D]   *[if it is so strong that] a wagon can go over it carrying stones.*

[E]   *They do not extend projections and balconies over the public domain.*

[F]   *But if one wanted, he brings in [his wall] into his own property and then projects [a balcony outward to his property line].*

[G]   *[If] one has purchased a courtyard, and in it are projections and balconies, lo, this one retains his right [to keep them as they are].*

[I.A]   [With reference to M. 3:11G,] if the projections or balconies fell down and one wants to reconstruct them—

[B]   R. Yohanan said, "He has given up his right to do so [and is deemed to have handed the space back to the public way]."

[C]   R. Simeon b. Laqish said, "He has not given up that right."

[D]   Now there is a Mishnah passage which supports the position of this party, and there is a Mishnah passage which supports the position of that party.

[E]   The Mishnah passage which supports the position of R. Yohanan is as follows:

[F]   *He who had a public way passing through his field and who took it away and gave [the public another path] along the side—what he has given he has given, but what was his does not pass back to him* [M. B.B. 6:7A–D].

[G]   The Mishnah passage which supports the position of R. Simeon b. Laqish is as follows:

[H]   *[If] one has purchased a courtyard, and in it are projections and balconies, lo, this one retains his right [to keep them as they are]* [M. 3:11G].

The Talmud fully works out the problem introduced at A, which is generated by the rule of M. 3:11G.

4:1

[A] *He who sells a house has not sold the extension,*

[B] *even though [the extension] opens into [the house],*

[C] *the room behind [the house],*

[D] *or the roof, if it has a parapet ten handbreadths high.*

[E] *R. Judah says, "If it has the shape of a door, even though it is not ten handbreadths high, it is not [deemed to have been] sold."*

[I.A] [14c] R. Nahum in the name of R. Hiyya bar Ba, "The rule [that the extension is not sold along with the house] applies in a case in which it is four cubits by four cubits with a height of ten cubits.

[B] "And it applies only if it is roofed over and sealed off."

[C] Said to them R. Zira, "And did R. Hiyya bar Aba provide for you this entire interpretation of the passage?"

[II.A] *And not the roof, if it has a parapet ten handbreadths high* [M. 4:1D].

[B] Is this the end of the matter [that there must be] a parapet? If the back walls of houses surrounded the area, [or] if there were pillars and posts on top of them, [would this also not constitute an adequate partition to indicate that the roof area is distinct from the house]?

[C] Let us derive the answer to that question from the following:

[D]   R. Judah says, "If it has the shape of a door, even though it is not ten handbreadths high, it is not deemed to have been sold" [M. 4:1E], [and the pillars do form the shape of a door].

[E]   They said, "And that [sages' position at M. 4:1D] is so if there is a parapet ten handbreadths high."

Judah's gloss, M. 4:1E, indicates that when the roof is so distinct from the house as to have a door, then even though it is not partitioned off by a ten-handbreadth-high wall, it nonetheless is deemed a distinct domain, in line with the basic theory of the pericope as a whole. Unit I contains a clarification of M. 4:1A, and unit II raises the question of whether Mishnah's rule is exclusive or whether similar arrangements produce the same result.

4:2

[A]   [Nor has he sold] the cistern,

[B]   or the cellar,

[C]   even though he wrote him [in the deed], "The depth and height."

[D]   "But [the seller] has to purchase [from the buyer] a right-of-way [to the cistern or the cellar]," the words of R. Aqiba.

[E]   And sages say, "He does not have to purchase a right-of-way."

[F]   And R. Aqiba concedes that when [the seller] said, "Except for these," he does not have to purchase a right-of-way for himself.

[G]   [If the seller then] sold [the cistern or cellar] to someone else,

[H]   R. Aqiba says, "[The new purchaser] does not have to buy a right-of-way for himself."

[I]   And sages say, "He has to buy a right-of-way for himself."

[I.A]   [If in the end one does not acquire the cistern or cellar,] for **what purpose does one write, "The depth and height"** [M. 4:2C]?

[B]   So that if [the purchaser] wishes to lower [the cellar], he
may lower it; if he wishes to raise it, he may raise it [T. B.B.
3:1H–J].

[II.A]   Rabbah bar R. Huna in the name of Rab: "The law is in accord
with R. Aqiba before us, for he is [the anonymous] rabbis [in a
saying involving] R. Hiyya. [Aqiba maintains that one sells in a
liberal spirit.]"

[B]   R. Zeira, R. Jeremiah in the name of Rab: "The law is in accord
with R. Aqiba vis-à-vis R. Hiyya,

[C]   "for he is 'the rabbis' of the Babylonians' [version of the
matter]."

[D]   There they say, "Admon and R. Aqiba. [Both of them say the
same thing, for at M. Ket. 13:7, Admon follows the principle of
Aqiba that if a right-of-way is lost through disuse, one need not
purchase a right-of-way]."

[E]   [Disagreeing with this view,] said R. La, "They differ from one
another when there has been no prior specification [of a right-of-
way, that is, as in the case before us]. [Admon will allow the
right-of-way only where there had been one already set forth,
which then was lost due to lack of use. But where there is no
such right-of-way established, Admon need not concur with
Aqiba's generous position.]

[F]   Now how shall we interpret this matter [to show that La, E, is
right]?

[G]   If it is certain that there is already a right-of-way, all parties concur that it is not necessary for him to purchase a right-of-way.

[H]   If it is certain that there is no right-of-way, all parties concur
that he has to purchase a right-of-way.

[I]   But thus must we interpret the matter: In a case in which the
matter has not been made explicit—

[J]   R. Aqiba says, "He does not have to purchase a right-of-way."

[K]   And sages say, "He has to purchase a right-of-way."

The extended gloss at M. 4:2D–H relates to a sale of the cistern
or cellar. Aqiba maintains that the seller must purchase from the

buyer of the property a right-of-way to these areas. Sages deem that right to have been implicit in the contract. If the seller of the house explicitly excluded from the sale the cistern or cellar, and the buyer of the house conceded, then, it follows, the buyer also has conceded the right-of-way, F. Reading G–I as a continuation of D–F, we proceed. If then the seller of the house sold the cistern or cellar to another party, that third party retains the interest of the original owner of the house, as he has preserved that interest in the procedures of D–F. Sages at the end see the third party as having to make his own arrangements, since, in their view, nothing in the original contract has by implication covered the right-of-way for yet another purchaser. Unit I then provides a minor clarification of Mishnah's language; unit II invokes a parallel case, at M. Ket. 13:7, and then raises the question of the distinction between the two cases. This is by asking whether Admon will concur with Aqiba's view. He clearly need not concur, for there is an obvious distinction between the issues of M. Ket. 13:7, where there had been a right of way which was lost, and M. B.B. 4:2, where there is no right of way established at all. Admon need not concede in this latter case that a presumptive claim is in existence. This discussion is somewhat allusive but poses no problems of interpretation.

4:3

[A]   *He who sells a house has sold the door, but not the key.*

[B]   *He has sold a permanent mortar, but not a movable one.*

[C]   *He has sold the convex millstone but not the concave millstone,*

[D]   *or the oven or the double stove.*

[E]   *When he said to him [in the deed], "It and everything which is in it,"*

[F]   *lo, all of them are sold.*

[I.A] Thus is the meaning of the Mishnah's rule: **He has sold the millstone which is hollowed out [of bedrock] but not the convex millstone** [T. B.B. 3:1B–C].

The Talmud revises M. 4:3C by reading it in line with Tosefta.

4:4

[A]   *He who sells a courtyard has sold the houses, cisterns, trenches, and caves,*

[B]   *but not the movables.*

[C]   *If he said to him, "It and everything which is in it,"*

[D]   *lo, all of them are sold.*

[E]   *One way or the other, he has not sold him the bathhouse or the olive-press which are in it.*

[F]   *R. Eliezer says, "He who sells the courtyard has sold only the open space of the courtyard."*

[I.A]   R. Isaac asked, "In the view of rabbis [vis-à-vis Eliezer], if one has sold the courtyard without further specification, has *he sold the houses, cisterns, trenches, and caves therein but not the movables,* or has he also sold the movables?"

[B]   R. Isaac asked, "In the view of R. Eliezer, "If one has sold the courtyard without further specification, he has sold him only the open space of the courtyard.

[C]   "If then he had said to him, '. . . it and whatever is in it,' has he *sold him the houses, cisterns, trenches, and caves, but not the movables,* or has he also sold the movables?"

[D]   Said R. Yohanan, "[Assuredly, M. 4:4A–B deals with a case in which one has sold the courtyard without further specification.] For I shall bring evidence for that view from the following statement of the house of Levi: 'If there were there courtyards open toward the inner space, they are deemed to have been sold. If they were open outward, they are not deemed to have been sold. If they opened both inward and outward, these and those are deemed to have been sold.' [This rule surely deals with a sale without further specification, for otherwise the question before the framer of the statement is not comprehensible. Had there been specification, surely the answer to the question dealt with here would have been known.]"

Isaac systematically asks penetrating questions for the exegesis of Mishnah. No answers are given.

4:5

[A]   *He who sells an olive-press has sold the vat, grindstone, and*
       posts.

[B]   *But he has not sold the pressing boards, wheel or beam.*

[C]   *If he said, "It and everything which is in it,"*

[D]   *lo, all of them are sold.*

[E]   *R. Eliezer says, "He who sells an olive-press has sold the beam."*

[I.A] The very definitive characteristic of this object is that if it has no
       beam, it is not to be called an olive-press—and yet you say this
       [that he has not sold the beam, M. 4:5B]!

[B]   Who has formulated this passage? It is R. Eleazar, for it has
       been taught in the name of R. Eleazar:

[C]   [Tosefta's version] **He who sells an olive-press has sold the**
       moulds, tanks, press beams, and lower millstones.

[D]   **But he has not sold the sacks, the packing bags, or the upper**
       millstones.

[E]   *But if he had said to him, "It and everything which is in it I sell*
       to you," lo, all of them are sold [M. 4:5C–D].

[F]   **But even though he has said to him, "It and everything which**
       is in it," he has not sold to him the cistern, ditch, extensions,
       cellars or caves which are in it.

[G]   **But if he said to him, "It and everything which is in it I sell to**
       you,"

[H]   **lo, all of them are sold.**

The Talmud once again cites Tosefta to clarify Mishnah.

4:6

[A]   *He who sells a bathhouse has not sold the boards, benches, or*
       hangings.

[B]   *If he said, "It and everything which is in it,"*

[C]   *lo, all of them are sold.*

[D]   *One way or the other, he has not sold the water jugs or woodsheds.*

[I.A]   It was taught: [Tosefta's version] **He who sells a bathhouse has sold the inner rooms, the outer rooms, the kettle room, the towel room, and the dressing room.**

[B]   **But he has not sold the kettles, the towels, or the [clothes] cupboards which are in it.**

[C]   R. Simeon b. Eleazar says, "The place of the gatekeeper is sold. The dressing room is not sold."

[D]   *But if he said to him, "It and everything which is in it I sell to you," lo, all of them are sold* [M. 4:6B–C].

[E]   **And even though he said to him, "It and everything which is in it I sell to you,"**

[F]   **he has not sold to him the water channels from which [the bathhouse] derives [water], whether [those used] in the dry season or the rainy season,**

[G]   **and also not the woodshed** [M. 4:6D].

[H]   **But if he had said to him, "The bathhouse and everything which is needed for making use of it do I sell to you,"**

[I]   **all of them are sold** [T. B.B. 3:3].

The Talmud simply cites Tosefta.

4:7

[A]   *He who sells a town has sold the houses, cisterns, ditches, caves, bathhouses, dovecotes, olive-presses, and irrigated fields,*

[B]   *but not the movables.*

[C]   *If he said to him, "It and everything which is in it,"*

[D]   *even though there are cattle and slaves in it,*

[E]   *lo, all of them are sold.*

[F]   *Rabban Simeon b. Gamaliel says, "He who sells a town has sold the town guard."*

[I.A]   It was taught:

[B]   [Tosefta's version] **He who sells a town—**

[C]   **Rabban Simeon b. Gamaliel [T. R. Judah] says, "The town guard (SNTR) is sold along with it [cf. M. 4:7F].**

[D]   **"But the town clerk ('WNQLMWS) is not sold along with it."**

[E]   **But if he had said to him, "It and everything which is in it I sell you,"**

[F]   **all of them are sold.**

[G]   **And even though he had said to him, "It and everything which is in it I sell to you,"**

[H]   **he has not sold him outlying parts or suburbs,**

[I]   **or the thickets which are set apart by themselves,**

[J]   **or the vivarium for wild beasts, fowl, and fish [T. B.B. 3:5].**

[K]   "Outlying parts" are valleys outside of town.

[L]   "Suburbs" are outlying villages.

[M]   As to the parts at the sea or river,

[N]   some Tannas teach that they are sold, and some, that they are not sold.

[O]   Said R. Hisda, "[There is no dispute among the Tannas.] The one who said that they are sold refers to the area within the town limits, and the one who said that they are not sold refers to the area beyond the town limits."

Again the Talmud cites Tosefta to clarify Mishnah, and then, at I.K–L, lightly glosses Tosefta. The rest is clear as given.

4:8   [in Leiden MS and *editio princeps* 4:8–11]

[A]   *He who sells a field has sold the stones which are needed for it, the canes in the vineyard which are needed for it, and the crop which is yet unplucked up from the ground;*

[B]   *a partition of reeds which covers less than a quarter-qab of space of ground, the watchman's house which is not fastened down with mortar, the carob which was not grafted, and the young sycamores.*

[C]   *But he has not sold the stones which are not needed for it, the canes in the vineyard which are not needed for it, the crop which has already been plucked up from the ground.*

[D]   *If he had said to him, "It and everything which is in it,"*

[E]   *lo, all of them are sold.*

[F]   *One way or the other, he has not sold to him a partition of reeds which covers a quarter-qab of space of ground, a watchman's house which is fastened down with mortar, a carob which was grafted, and cropped sycamores;*

[G]   *[or] a cistern, winepress, or dovecote,*

[H]   *whether they are lying waste or in use.*

[I]   *"And [the seller] needs to purchase [from the buyer] a right-of-way," the words of R. Aqiba.*

[J]   *And sages say, "He does not have to."*

[K]   *And R. Aqiba concedes that, when [the seller] said to him, "Except for these," he does not have to buy himself a right-of-way.*

[L]   *[If] he sold them to someone else,*

[M]   *R. Aqiba says, "[The new purchaser] does not have to buy a right-of-way for himself."*

[N]   *And sages say, "He has to buy a right-of-way for himself."*

[O]   *Under what circumstances?*

[P]   *In the case of one who sells [the aforelisted properties].*

[Q]   *But in the case of one who gives a gift,*

[R]   *he [willingly] hands over all of them.*

[S]   *Brothers who divided [an estate]—*

[T]   *once they have acquired possession of a field, they have acquired possession of all of them [and no longer may retract].*

[U]   *He who lays hold of the property of a deceased proselyte [lacking Israelite heirs],*

[V]   *once he has acquired possession of a field, has acquired possession of all of them.*

[W]   *He who declares a field sanctified has declared all of them sanctified.*

[X]   *R. Simeon says, "He who declares a field sanctified has declared sanctified only the carob which is grafted and cropped sycamores."*

[I.A]   [As to the canes in the vineyard which are needed for it,] members of the house of R. Yannai say, "[The reference is] to those which are divided up among the vines. [Those are the ones deemed sold, since they are needed for the vines.]"

[II.A]   R. Hiyya the Great asked, "If there were there unattached posts [to be] cut, [are all of them needful]?"

[B]   R. Isaac bar Tabelai asked, "If there were there [in a house] unattached sheets of marble for walls, [are they needful]?"

[C]   R. Yudan bar R. Ishmael asked, "If there were there unattached bricks for windows, [are they needful]?"

[III.A]   R. Hiyya in the name of R. Yohanan: "If there is there a furrow six by six, bearing its own distinctive name [e.g., deemed separate from the other furrows of a field], it is not sold."

[IV.A]   Said R. Yohanan, "He who buys a cropped sycamore in the field of his fellow—[such a case is subject] to the dispute of R. Ishmael b. R. Yosé and rabbis.

[B]   "R. Ishmael b. R. Yosé says, 'He also has purchased the ground [on which the sycamore is standing, as in the case of buying three trees].'

[C]   "And rabbis [14d] say, 'He has not purchased the ground [on which the sycamore is standing].'"

[D]   R. Hiyya bar Vava asked, "If one sold him an entire field, but left for himself a cropped sycamore—

[E]   "in the view of R. Ishmael b. R. Yosé, the seller has retained ownership of the land [on which the tree is standing] [PM].

[F]   "In the opinion of rabbis, he has not acquired the land [thereon]."

[G]   R. Isaac bar Tabelai asked, "If one has sold to him, 'Every tree and the olive tree in such and such a place'—are all of the olive trees which are located in that place deemed to have been sold?"

[H]   [With reference to having sold with a field a partition of reeds which covers less than a quarter-*qab* of space of ground, M. 4:8B,] R. Yudan bar Ishmael asked, "He who purchases three sets of reeds [less than a quarter-*qab* of space of ground], has he purchased also the largest cedar tree in the Land of Israel? [That is, even though the reed partition is less than the specified size, if there were within that area a very large tree, would we deem the tree to have been sold, despite its size and distinctiveness]?"

[V.A]   *Under what circumstances? In the case of one who sells the afore-listed properties. But in the case of one who gives a gift, he willingly hands over all of them* [M. 4:8/O–R].

[B]   And what is the difference between selling and giving as a gift?

[C]   R. Ba bar Tabelai in the name of Rab: "For it is the way of one who gives a gift to give in a liberal spirit."

[D]   R. Samuel bar Nahman in the name of R. Jonathan: "For it is the way of one who purchases to pay close attention to detail."

[E]   What is the practical difference between these two [explanations]?

[F]   It is the case of one who consecrates [a property].

[G]   He who says that it is the way of one who gives a gift to give in a liberal spirit holds that he who consecrates property does so in a liberal spirit as well.

[H]   And one who says that it is the way of one who purchases to pay close attention to detail—will he hold the same in the case of one who consecrates property? [For the recipient of a gift or the Temple treasurer is not apt to look too closely at the gift.] [This question is not answered, and the text breaks off here.]

[VI.A]   [Supply, following PM: R. Eleazar asked, Does the distinction between selling and giving, at M. 4:8/O, apply to all the cases in such wise that the dispute about purchasing a right-of-way, between Aqiba and sages, pertains to every item in the antecedent catalogue? Or does the distinction between selling and giving apply only to the items listed at the outset, M. 4:8A–B, in which case, in *these* cases only, there is a dispute about purchasing a right-of-way? That is, at the outset we list various items not sold along with a field. We further have the dispute about whether or not one has to purchase a right-of-way. Now do we hold that if one has sold the stated items, one does have to purchase a right-of-way, while if one gives them as a gift, one does not have to purchase a right-of-way? Or perhaps the distinction between purchasing and acquiring as a gift applies only to the items listed at the outset. Then that distinction has nothing to do with whether or not one must purchase a right-of-way.] Let us derive the answer from the following:

[B]   Brothers who divided an inheritance—each has [to purchase] a right-of-way from the other. [From this it follows that the division does not take place in a liberal spirit. And yet here the context is property acquired as a gift. It follows that the distinction between purchase and gift applies only to the matters listed at the outset of M. 4:8.]

[C]   And there are those who wish to say, "Thus said R. Eleazar: *'Brothers who divided an estate—once they have acquired possession of a field, they have acquired possession of all of them'* [M. 4:8S–T], [so that Eleazar himself answers his question]. [Citing the pericope in the Mishnah indicates that property received as a gift does not come in a liberal spirit.]"

[VII.A]   *He who lays hold of the property of a deceased proselyte [lacking Israelite heirs], once he has acquired possession of a field, he has acquired possession of all of them. He who declares a field sanctified has declared all of them sanctified. R. Simeon says, "He who declares a field sanctified has declared sanctified only the carob which is grafted and cropped sycamores"* [M. 4:8U–X].

[B]   [The reason for the position of R. Simeon] is that they draw sustenance from ground which has been consecrated [so they too are deemed consecrated].

[C]   Is the reason that he has left himself a path? [That is, is it Simeon's position that he has declared the property consecrated only in a niggardly spirit? He has left himself a right-of-way in the field. So in fact it is only the carob and sycamore that he has consecrated. This is for the reason just now stated, namely, because they derive sustenance from the consecrated field. Or does R. Simeon maintain that, by consecrating these trees, he has in fact consecrated the field and has left himself no right-of-way in the field at all?]

[D]   Is it only if he has not left himself a right of way in the field?! [How can that be a consideration? The trees still draw sustenance from somewhere!]

[E]   But the reason is only that they draw sustenance from the consecrated field [and that is the sole pertinent reason].

Unit **II** presents a set of topics for possible discussion, but all are truncated, a trait of the unit before us in general. Unit **III** consists of a single observation. Unit **IV** does amplify the law given in Mishnah. At issue is whether the trees specified in Mishnah carry with them the ground on which they stand. This question is nicely spelled out, with both possible answers explored adequately. Unit **IV** further contains materials for discussion left undeveloped. Unit **V** provides a fine example of the Talmud at its best, asking an important question, eliciting two distinct reasons, then spelling out the difference consequent upon each of the stated reasons. Unit **VI** is reconstructed following PM, and at **VI.**C we find justification for PM's adoption of an earlier commentator's proposal for a reconstruction. Unit **VII** is clear as given. In all the Talmud here gives us a promise of what could have been a long and sustained discourse upon an important Mishnah-pericope, but only at a few points is that promise kept.

5 Yerushalmi Baba Batra
Chapter Five

5:1 [In Leiden MS and *editio princeps* 5:1–4]

[A] *He who sells a ship has sold the mast, sail, and anchor,*

[B] *and whatever steers it.*

[C] *But he has not sold the slaves, packing bags, or lading.*

[D] *And if [the seller] had said to [the buyer,] "It and everything which is in it," lo, all of them are sold.*

[E] *[If] he sold the wagon, he has not sold the mules.*

[F] *[If] he sold the mules, he has not sold the wagon.*

[G] *[If] he sold the yoke, he has not sold the oxen.*

[H] *[If] he sold the oxen, he has not sold the yoke.*

[I] *R. Judah says, "The price tells all."*

[J] *How so?*

[K] *[If] he said to him, "Sell me your yoke for two hundred zuz,"*

[L] *the facts are perfectly clear,*

[M] *for there is no yoke worth two hundred zuz.*

[N] *And sages say, "The price proves nothing."*

[O] *He who sells an ass has not sold its trappings.*

[P] *Nahum the Mede says, "He has sold its trappings."*

[Q] *R. Judah says, "Sometimes they are sold, and sometimes they are not sold."*

[R]   *How so?*

[S]   *[If] there was an ass before him, with its trappings on it, and he said to him, "Sell me this ass of yours,"*

[T]   *lo, its trappings are sold.*

[U]   *[If he had said, "Sell me] that ass of yours," its trappings are not sold.*

[V]   *He who sells an ass has sold the foal.*

[W]   *[If] he sold the cow, he has not sold its offspring.*

[X]   *[If] he sold a dungheap, he has sold the dung on it.*

[Y]   *[If] he sold a cistern, he has sold its water.*

[Z]   *[If] he sold a beehive, he has sold the bees.*

[AA]   *[If] he has sold the dovecote, he has sold the pigeons.*

[BB]   *He who purchases "the fruit of a dovecote" from his fellow lets go the first pair that are hatched.*

[CC]   *[If he bought] "the fruit of a beehive," he takes three swarms, and then [the seller] makes the rest sterile.*

[DD]   *[If he bought] honeycombs, he leaves two honeycombs.*

[EE]   *[If he bought] olive trees to cut down, he leaves two shoots.*

[I.A]   [15a] [Tosefta's version] It was taught: **He who sells a ship has sold the wooden implements and the water tank on it.**

[B]   **But he has not sold the deck cabins, the anchor** [vs. M. B.B. 5:1A], **the yard, or the lighter.**

[C]   **Sumkhos says, "He has sold the lighter"** [T. B.B. 4:1A–C].

[II.A]   The unstipulated conditions [which apply to transactions even when not made explicit] laid down by Joshua—

[B]   R. Levi b. Biri in the name of R. Joshua b. Levi: "[They are] four [in all]."

[C]   (1) People may gather grass anywhere, except for a field of fenugreek, which is prohibited as theft.

[D]   There we have learned: *[If in a crop of grain aftergrowths of wood sprang up—so too in the place of threshing floors if many*

kinds sprang up;] so too if fenugreek made weeds to spring up,
he is not bound to weed them out. [But if he has weeded them
or cropped them, they say to him, "Uproot them all, except for
one kind," so as to avoid violating the law against mixed seeds"
(M. Kil. 2:5).]

[E]   Thus does the cited Mishnah state, that they do not obligate the
man to uproot them [because these grasses are destructive and
will be uprooted in any event].

[F]   Now in accord with the stipulation imputed to Joshua, it was
stated, "People may gather grass anywhere, except for a field of
fenugreek, which is prohibited as theft."

[G]   And now there is a statement that one does not want that sort of
grass at all. [Hence there is a contradiction between the two
rules.]

[H]   Thus one may say, "There [in the case of Joshua's stipulation], it
is a case in which one sowed them for spikes, while here [at M.
Kil. 2:5], it is a case in which one sowed them for seed."

[I]   Now do you wish to say that Joshua made a stipulation covering
people who violate the law [for at M. Kil. 2:5, the grasses in
fact constitute mixed seeds, so too in the other field, and, in the
latter instance, Joshua has provided a remedy so that people will
not steal the grasses? But they should not be there to begin
with!]

[J]   R. Samuel bar Nahman in the name of R. Jonathan: "It is a case
in which the man plans to pluck them, and it is as if they have
been uprooted and lie before him. [Of course, the man will ultimately pluck them, and does not want to keep them in the field.
One should not collect grasses from such a field, since the owner
wants them for himself and will not preserve a situation of
mixed seeds in his field.]"

[K]   And why not say the same thing in the case of mixed seeds in a
vineyard? [That is, if there are mixed seeds in a vineyard, they
too should be forbidden by reason of theft, since the man wants
them and certainly will pluck them, and consequently they are
treated as if they have already have been plucked out of the vineyard. The answer is, that is indeed the case.]

[L]   For R. Yannai has said, "All growths are prohibited, except for those which grow up in an uncultivated field, a fallow field, a vineyard, and a field planted in with seed.

[M] "In an uncultivated field—because the owner pays no attention to the growth anyhow.

[N] "In a fallow field—because the owner wants to prepare the field for plowing anyhow.

[O] "In a vineyard—so that the presence of the mixed seeds will not prohibit use of the vineyard [and hence wants them removed = K].

[P] "In a field planted with seed—for the owner does not want the growths anyhow.

[Q] "And if you say that he wants them, then they are deemed to have been plucked up and laid before him anyhow."

[R] There we have learned: *He who finds a corpse in the first instance lying in usual fashion removes it and the earth affected by it. [If he found two, he removes them and the earth surrounding them. If he found three, if there are between one and the other from four to eight cubits, lo, this is deemed a graveyard* (M. Naz. 9:3A–E).]

[S] Said R. Hisda, "That is to say that in the case of a neglected corpse, one is permitted to move it from its place.

[T] "For we have learned, *'He removes it and the earth affected by it.'*"

[U] And how much [dirt does one remove]?

[V] R. Samuel in the name of R. Jonathan: "Up to three fingerbreadths, the place to which the dripping blood [from the corpse] descends."

[W] Said R. Zeira, "It is not reasonable. [That is, the conclusion drawn from the cited pericope by Hisda is wrong.]

[X] "For it is prohibited to move a neglected corpse. For if you say that it is permitted to move it, these [the three referred to later on in the same passage]—since they cause the loss of the entire field, is it not an argument a fortiori that it is permitted to move them [from their place]? [But that is not the provision of the Mishnah-pericope!]

[Y] "Hence, what was clear to the master who taught the cited passage is that it is prohibited to move a neglected corpse from its place. On that account it was necessary to teach the law [that if one did so, he also removes the dirt around the corpse]. [But one is not permitted to do so (PM).]"

[Z] Said R. Hisda, "The Mishnah before us accords with the opinion of the one who maintains that it is permitted to move a neglected corpse.

[AA] "But I say that [in the present case], the corpse was buried in a private path [with permission of the owner of the path, and the corpse would be moved later on]."

[BB] And why should we hesitate to say that it was a neglected corpse?

[CC] [The answer is that] neglected corpses are not commonly found lying around.

[DD] [We now return to the stipulations assigned to the authority of Joshua, A.] [It is permitted] for people to traverse private paths from the harvest time until the time at which the latter rains fall.

[EE] And anywhere people may take plants for themselves, except olives and grapes—

[FF] in the case of an olive plant, from the newest of the new and the oldest of the old [in which case it is not yet productive or is past producing, so it is permitted to take growths].

[GG] But in the case of an olive plant in the shape of a whip even in the case of the newest of the new, it is prohibited to do so.

[HH] R. Tanhum of Kefar Gavan in the name of R. Eleazar b. R. Yosé: "They are four [stipulations, = A].

[II] (1) "They gather grass anywhere, on condition that one does not pull up the grass by the roots.

[JJ] (2) "And people may relieve themselves on the other side of a wall [anywhere]."

[KK] R. Eleazar b. R. Yosé in the name of R. Tanhum: "That applies to a place in which one may sneeze without being heard [but in a more populated area, one may not relieve himself]."

[LL]   (3) "And they may pasture a flock in forest, even a flock belonging to the tribe of Judah in the territory of the tribe of Naftali.

[MM]   ("And they assign to Naphtali a complete strip of land south of the lake, as it is said, 'O Naphtali, satisfied with favor and full of the blessing of the Lord, possess the lake and the south'" [Deut. 33:23], the words of R. Yosé the Galilean.

[NN]   R. Aqiba says, "The reference to the sea here is to the sea of Samkho, and the reference to the south refers to the sea of Tiberias [and it has nothing to do with a strip of land south of the sea]."

[OO]   (4) And people may walk along the sides of the road [in a field to avoid the center of the road when there is traffic on it].

[PP]   R. Judah in the name of Rab: "Even if it is a field full of saffron [which is very costly and valuable]."

[QQ]   Does one have to pay for damages done thereby or not?

[RR]   From that which R. Judah said, "Even if it is a field full of saffron," one may conclude that one indeed has to pay damages.

[SS]   Said R. La, "Since R. Judah said, 'Even if it is a field full of saffron,' one must infer that one does not have to pay damages."

[TT]   And one cannot go too far into the field.

[UU]   And we derive that inference from the following [story]:

[VV]   M^cSH B (W): Rabban Gamaliel and R. Joshua were walking along the way, and they saw Judah b. Pappos drawing near and coming toward them. Said Rabban Gamaliel to R. Joshua, "Who is this person who is showing off his piety by pointing to himself?"

[WW]   He said to him, "It is Judah b. Pappos. Whatever he does is for the sake of Heaven." [One need not try to avoid him, he is an honest man.]

[III.A]   R. Samuel in the name of R. Jonathan: "He who wants to build a town at the outset—they assign to him four paths, in four directions [as a right-of-way]."

[B]   R. Haninah raised the question before R. Mana, "What is the meaning of this requirement that he be assigned a right of way

in all four points of the compass? Is it [in breadth] from four
cubits to eight or from eight to sixteen?"

[C] He said to him, "It is from eight to sixteen, so that two wagons
can pass side by side going in opposite directions."

None of this has any bearing whatsoever on the Mishnah-
pericope before us. Unit **II**, on unstated stipulations, presum-
ably is relevant because the conception of Joshua's four unstated
stipulations is parallel to the notion of unstated stipulations
which occupies Mishnah.

5:2   [In Leiden MS and *editio princeps* 5:5–6]

[A] *He who buys two trees in his fellow's field,*

[B] *lo, this party has not bought the ground [on which they are
growing].*

[C] *R. Meir says, "He has bought the ground."*

[D] *[If] they grew up, [the landowner] may not trim them.*

[E] *What sprouts from the stem belongs to [the purchaser],*

[F] *[but what sprouts] from the roots belongs to the owner of the
land.*

[G] *And if [the trees] died, [the owner of the trees] has no claim on
the land.*

[H] *[If] he bought three, he has [also] bought the ground [on which
they are growing].*

[I] *[If] they grew up, [the landowner] may trim them.*

[J] *And what sprouts both from the stem and from the roots belongs to [the purchaser].*

[K] *And if [the trees] died, he has a claim on the land.*

[I.A] Members of the house of R. Yannai say, "That which is in the
shade—this is the root. That which is open to the sun—this is
the stem" [M. 5:2E–F].

[B] R. Hama bar Uqbah in the name of R. Yosé: "That which grows up from its roots and from its stem—this is assigned the status of the root.

[C] "That which grows up from its stem and not from its roots—this is assigned the status of the tree."

[II.A] Said R. Yohanan, "He who purchases three trees [M. 5:2H] has purchased the land between them, under them, and outside of them to the breadth of a tree trimmer and his basket."

[B] Said R. Eleazar, "He does not have a right of way, [and yet] does he have a claim on land around the tree to the breadth of the space required for a tree trimmer and his basket?"

Mishnah's two sets of four rulings (ignoring Meir's contrary view, which would then stand in the way of A–B, D–G), explain the consequences of owning the tree but not the ground under it. What the person has bought is the produce of the tree and the right to cut the tree down. The landowner may not trim a tree in the former case, even though the branches shadow his land. The theory is that, just as he has let out his land for the use of the tree, so he has let it out for the tree's branches. There is no landmark. What sprouts from the roots grows in land owned by the landowner, E–F. G simply repeats B. If the purchase involves three trees, the land underneath is deemed purchased also. Both units of the Talmud gloss Mishnah, as indicated. **II**.B rejects **II**.A.

5:3   [In Leiden MS and *editio princeps* 5:7]

[A]   *He who sells the head [in the case of] large cattle has not sold the feet.*

[B]   *[If] he sold the feet, he has not sold the head.*

[C]   *[If] he sold the lungs, he has not sold the liver.*

[D]   *[If] he sold the liver, he has not sold the lungs.*

[E]   *But in the case of a small beast,*

[F]   *[If] he has sold the head, he has sold the feet.*

[G]   *[If] he has sold the feet, he has not sold the head.*

[H]   *[If] he has sold the lungs, he has sold the liver.*

[I]   *[If] he has sold the liver, he has not sold the lungs.*

[I.A] R. Isaac asked, "If one has sold half the head [of a small beast, M. 5:3E–F], has he sold half the feet?

[B]   "If he sold half the lungs, has he sold half the liver?"

[C]   [Delete: If he sold half the lungs—]

[D]   Let us derive the answer to this question from the following:

[E]   **If one sold him the hand as it is [not by weight] and the head as it is and the intestines as they are, he gives them to a priest. And he does not deduct from what he pays the butcher the cost thereof** [T. Hul. 9:8; cf. M. Hul. 10:3H]. *If he purchased it from him by weight, he gives them to the priest. But he deducts their value from what he pays the butcher* [M. Hul. 10:3I]. [Now if you maintain that if one has sold half the head, he has not sold half the feet, why should the cited passage differentiate between purchase as is and purchase by weight? Even if purchased as is, we could deduct the value from the price, e.g., if one has sold the shoulder with the foot or the cheeks with the head or the maw with the intestines. It must follow that if one has sold him half the head, he also has sold half the feet (PM).]

Isaac's question is meant to sharpen the picture of Mishnah's rule, and the answer is clear as spelled out.

5:4   [In Leiden MS and *editio princeps* 5:8–10]

[A]   *There are four rules in the case of those who sell:*

[B]   *[If] one has sold good wheat and it turns out to be bad, the purchaser has the power to retract.*

[C]   *[If one has sold] bad wheat and it turns out to be good, the seller has the power to retract.*

[D]   *[If he has claimed to sell] bad wheat, and it turns out to be bad,*

[E]   *[or if he claimed to sell] good wheat and it turns out to be good,*

[F]   *neither one of them has the power to retract.*

[G]   *[If one sold it as] dark-colored, and it turns out to be white,*

[H]   *white, and it turned out to be dark,*

[I]   *olive wood, and it turned out to be sycamore wood,*

[J]   *sycamore wood, and it turned out to be olive wood,*

[K]   *wine, and it turned out to be vinegar,*

[L]   *vinegar, and it turned out to be wine,*

[M]   *both parties have the power to retract.*

[N]   *He who sells produce to his fellow—*

[O]   *[if the buyer] drew it but did not measure it, he has acquired possession of it.*

[P]   *[If] he measured it but did not draw it [to himself], he has not acquired possession.*

[Q]   *If he is smart, he will rent the place [in which the produce is located].*

[R]   *He who purchases flax from his fellow—*

[S]   *lo, this one has not acquired possession until he moves it from one place to another.*

[T]   *But if it was attached to the ground and he has plucked any small quantity of it, he has acquired possession.*

[U]   *He who sells wine or oil to his fellow,*

[V]   *and [the price] rose or fell,*

[W]   *if this took place before the measure [belonging to the purchaser] had been filled up, [the price advantage goes] to the seller.*

[X]   *[If this took place] after the measure had been filled up, [the price advantage goes] to the purchaser.*

[Y]   *And if there was a middleman between them,*

[Z]   *[and] the jar was broken,*

[AA]   *it is broken [to the disadvantage of] the middleman.*

[BB]   *[After emptying the measure, the seller] is liable to let three drops drip.*

[CC]   *[If thereafter] he turned the measure over and drained it, lo, [what is drained off] goes to the seller.*

[DD]   *But the shopkeeper is not liable to let three more drops drip.*

[EE]   *R. Judah says, "If it is the eve of the Sabbath at dusk, he is exempt."*

[I.A]   [With reference to M. 5:4W: *If this took place before the measure belonging to the purchaser had been filled up, the price advantage goes to the seller; if afterward, to the purchaser:*] How so? [Why is the point of filling up the measure a criterion at all?]

[B]   If the measure belonged to the seller, the profit presumptively is assigned to the seller.

[C]   If it belonged to the purchaser, the profit presumptively belongs to the purchaser, [and that is the case even if the measure has been filled up].

[D]   R. Judah in the name of Samuel, R. La in the name of R. Judah b. Rabbi: "Thus does the Mishnah speak, namely, of a case in which the measure belonged to a third party."

[II.A]   *R. Judah says, "If it is the eve of the Sabbath at dusk, he is exempt* [M. 5:4EE], because it is a matter of choice [that he let three more drops drip]."

[B]   And sages say, "One way or the other, he is liable [since it is not a matter of choice]."

[III.A]   What is the reason [that, if the jar was broken, it is broken to the disadvantage of the middleman (M. 5:4Y–AA)]?

[B]   Said R. Yudan, "'If it was rented out, it came for its rent' (Ex. 22:14). [That is, the middleman is in the status of a paid bailee and so is liable if the measure is broken.]"

It is the act of drawing to oneself, M. 5:4N–P, which effects possession in the case of movables, N–P. Merely measuring out what is to be purchased has no effect. The buyer does well to

rent the place in which what he purchases is located, Q, so that
the seller cannot retract. Since, it is assumed, the measure at M.
5:4U, belongs to the purchaser, once the wine or oil has been
poured into the measure, the purchaser is deemed to have taken
possession of it; in line with what already has been said, W–X
follow. The middleman is equivalent to a paid bailee and so
makes up any loss which occurs, Y–AA. To make sure that the
measure is fully empty, BB–CC, the seller has to let a few more
drops fall into the utensil held by the purchaser. Once this is
done, what is drained out of the seller's measure is retained by
him. The retailer does not have to follow this procedure; he is
assumed to be busy with many other customers. Judah, EE,
then invokes the same principle for the wholesaler, BB, when he
too is occupied and in a hurry. Unit **I** raises the necessary question in clarification of M. 5:4W. Unit **II** amplifies Judah's reasoning at the indicated passage. In assigning the discourse of
unit **III** to M. 5:4Y–AA, I follow PM's alternative view of the
passage.

5:5   [In Leiden MS and *editio princeps* 5:11–13]

[A]   *He who sends his child to the storekeeper with a pondion in his*
        hand,

[B]   *and [the storekeeper] measured out for him an issar's worth of*
        oil [half a pondion] and gave him an issar [in change],

[C]   *and [the child] broke the flask or lost the issar [of change]—*

[D]   *the storekeeper is liable [to make it up].*

[E]   *R. Judah declares him exempt,*

[F]   *for it was with the stipulation [that the father will bear liability]*
        that he had sent him.

[G]   *But sages [A–D] concur with R. Judah,*

[H]   *that when the flask was in the child's hand, and the storekeeper*
        measured out [oil] into it, the storekeeper is exempt.

[I]   *A wholesaler must clean off his measures once every thirty days,*

[J]   *and a householder once every twelve months.*

[K]   *Rabban Simeon b. Gamaliel says, "Matters are just the opposite."*

[L]   *The storekeeper cleans off his measures twice a week, polishes his weights once a week, and cleans his scales after each and every weighing.*

[M]   *Said Rabban Simeon b. Gamaliel, "Under what circumstances?*

[N]   *"In the case of liquid measures.*

[O]   *"But in the case of dry measures, it is not necessary."*

[P]   *And [a shopkeeper] is liable to let the scales go down by a hand-breadth [to the buyer's advantage].*

[Q]   *[If] he was measuring out for him exactly, he has to give him an overweight—*

[R]   *one part in ten for liquid measure,*

[S]   *one part in twenty for dry measure.*

[T]   *In a place in which they are accustomed to measure with small measures, one must not measure with large measures;*

[U]   *[. . .] with large ones, one must not measure with small;*

[V]   *[in a place in which it is customary] to smooth down [what is in the measure], one should not heap it up;*

[W]   *[. . .] to heap it up, one should not smooth it down.*

[I.A] Said R. Ba bar Mamal, "[Regarding the relationship between the measures by tenths at M. 5:5Q–S and the measure of an excess of a handbreadth at M. 5:5P], when one is weighing out produce by tenths, one is liable [as the counterpart] to let the scales down by a handbreadth [to the buyer's advantage]. [So the one measure is tantamount to the other.]"

[II.A] It is written, "[You shall do no wrong in judgment, in measures of length, weight, or quantity;] you shall have just balances, just weights, a just ephah, and a just hin: [I am the Lord your God who brought you out of the land of Egypt]" (Lev. 19:35–36).

[B]   On the basis of the cited passage, sages have stated, "In any religious duty alongside of which the reward for doing that duty is specified, a court is not responsible [for the enforcement of that religious duty]. [For the individual merely gives up the specified reward as penalty for not doing the specified duty.]"

[C]   "You shall not have in your bag two kinds of weights, a large and a small. . . . A full and just weight you shall have, a full and just measure you shall have . . ." (Deut. 25:13–15)—meaning that you should appoint a market supervisor to oversee such a matter. [So the court does have to supervise the enforcement of the law], and yet you say what has been said above?

[D]   Said R. Bun bar Hiyya, "This is the meaning of the cited passage. In the case of any religious duty, the reward of which is specified alongside, a court is not *punished* on account [of neglecting to enforce that religious duty]. [But the court nonetheless is responsible for enforcing it.]"

[E]   The exilarch appointed Rab as market supervisor. [15b] Rab enforced the law in regard to measures but not in regard to weights. The exilarch threw him into prison. Rab Qarna came to him.

[F]   [Rab] said to him, "The market supervisor of which [sages] have spoken is one for measures and not for weights."

[G]   He said to him, "And lo, you have taught, 'The market supervisor oversees both measures and weights.'"

[H]   He said to him, "Go and instruct them: 'The market supervisor of which they have spoken is for measures and *not* for weights.'"

[I]   He went and said to them, "Here is someone who teaches the law as a preserve of Ahina-dates [late and inferior ones, so Jastrow, p. 20a, s.v. 'HYN'], and yet they throw him into prison!"

The Talmud deals only with M. 5:5Lff. There is no pretense at treating Mishnah beyond unit **I**. The relevance of the other materials is clear. The meaning of **II.I** is taken from Jastrow, as indicated.

6 Yerushalmi Baba Batra
Chapter Six

6:1   [In Leiden MS and *editio princeps* 6:1–2]

[A]   *He who sells produce [consisting of grain] to his fellow [not specifying whether it is for food or for seed],*

[B]   *and [the seed] did not sprout,*

[C]   *and even if it was flax seed,*

[D]   *he is not liable to make it up,*

[E]   *Rabban Simeon b. Gamaliel says, "[If he sold] garden seed which is not suitable for eating, he is liable to make it up."*

[F]   *He who sells produce to his fellow—*

[G]   *lo, [the buyer] must agree to receive a quarter-qab of spoiled produce per seah.*

[H]   *(1) [If he bought] figs, he must agree to accept ten maggoty ones per hundred.*

[I]   *(2) [If he bought] a cellar of wine, he must agree to accept ten sour jars per hundred.*

[J]   *(3) [If he bought] jars in Sharon, he must agree to accept ten faulty ones per hundred.*

[K]   *He who sells wine to his fellow, and it went sour, is not liable to make it up.*

[L]   *But if it was known that his wine would turn sour, lo, this is deemed a purchase made in error.*

[M]   *If he had said to him, "I'm selling you spiced wine,"*

[N] *he is liable to guarantee it [and make it up if it goes sour] up to Pentecost.*

[O] *[If he said it is] old [wine, it must be] last year's.*

[P] *[If he said it is] vintage-old, [it must be] from the year before last.*

[I.A] It was taught: *He who sells produce to his fellow, and [the seed] did not sprout, and even if it was flax seed is not liable to make it up [M. 6:1A–D],*

[B] but if he had stipulated with him at the outset that it was for seed, he is liable to make it up.

[C] What does [the vendor] pay out in compensation to him?

[D] The cost of the seed.

[E] And there are those who say, "He pays him the cost of his outlay [in planting the seed in addition to the cost of the seed]."

[II.A] In the present instance, we note, one accepts a [quarter-*qab* of spoiled produce per *seah*] [M. 6:1G],

[B] while there one must remove it [at M. Kil. 2:1: *If in a seah of seed there is a quarter-qab of another kind, this must be lessened*]. [Accordingly, the quarter-*qab* per *seah* is not deemed null in the much larger quantity, but is taken into account. Here it is null.]

[C] In the present case, one accepts maggoty ones, but there, one deals with another kind entirely.

[D] Here one accepts the maggoty ones upon delivery [not transported from one place to another]. [That is, e.g., wine is poured out from top to bottom, and the buyer gets what is poured out. But in the other case, the seed is deemed to have gotten mixed up] as the produce was moved from place to place.

[E] In the present context, R. Simeon agrees [to the rule, since he is not cited as differing from the stated rule], while there [at M. Kil. 2:1] R. Simeon says, "They are two distinct kinds and are not deemed to join together." [Simeon invokes the rule at M. Kil. 2:1 only if the seeds are of a single variety. But here he concedes that if the refuse is of some other variety, it still is deemed null. The solution to all these contrasts is simply that the rules governing mixed seeds are more strict than those governing the sale of produce in the present setting.]

[**III**.A] R. Hiyya bar Ba asked, "A *seah* of produce in the status of heave offering which fell into a hundred in the status of unconsecrated food [PM]—

[B] "As to a priest and an Israelite—

[C] "what is the law governing their dividing the return [on the seed]? [The heave offering is deemed null in a mixture of one hundred and one parts of unconsecrated food to one of heave offering. One has to remove a *seah* in the status of heave offering from the mixture and give it to a priest. If then one did not do so but planted the entire mixture, then what comes up from the seed containing heave offering is deemed to be produce in the status of unconsecrated food. But now we ask whether one has to hand over to a priest the profit accruing to that *seah* in proportion to the whole crop, or whether it is deemed null entirely. So we want to know whether the priest has any claim on the profit of the mixture of seed in the status of heave offering with ordinary seed when it produces a crop.]

[D] R. Isaac bar Tabelai asked, "A *seah* of wheat which fell into a hundred [*seah*s] of barley [PM]—

[E] "as to a seller and a buyer—

[F] "what is the law governing their dividing the remainder?" [In this case, one has sold a hundred *seah*s of barley. A single *seah* of wheat, which is of greater value, has fallen into the barley. Does the purchaser have to return to the seller the extra *seah*, which the seller did not sell to him? And if so, does he return it to him from this mixture, or does he have to go and give back only wheat? Now the purchaser may say, "I do not want your wheat." Is the vendor then supposed to go and pick out the grains of wheat, which are now mixed with the barley? So the question is whether they then divide the remainder, that is, the extra *seah* of wheat which has fallen in.]

[G] Said R. Bun bar Hiyya, "Let us derive the answer to the question from the following rule:

[H] "'He who picks out pebbles from the sheaves of his fellow is liable to appease him [by making up the cost].' [He has to pay in proportion to the wheat sheaves, which are diminished in volume by his picking out the refuse, for he thereby diminishes the volume of the sheaves and hence deprives the owner of what he can have sold them for. The purchaser has, after all, to accept a quarter-*qab* of such refuse per *seah*. But the one who has picked up the refuse cannot put it back into the sheaves, since it would be a deliberate act of adulteration. This yields the principle that what is mixed together in the sheaves is deemed part of the sheaves, of the same character as the sheaves themselves. Now, to deal with our problem, when a *seah* of wheat is mixed up with a sheaf of barley, one cannot pick out the wheat. So the wheat is deemed of the same species as the rest of what is in the sheaf, namely, the barley. The owner of the barley returns a *seah* of the sheaf as is.]"

[I]   R. Bun bar Kahana said, "This applies to a case in which one says, 'Make it into a pile and I shall buy it.' But if they were in a pile at the outset, it is not in such a case [that one has to pay back a *seah* at all]. [Since this is the condition in which the sheaves were sold anyhow, the purchaser need return nothing. This is what he assumed he had bought all along.]"

[IV.A] It was taught: **[R. Simeon b. Eleazar says,] "'A hundred jars I am selling to you'—he is liable to hand over to him wine as good as the average wine which is sold in that locale"** [T. B.B. 6:8].

[B]   **"A hundred jars of wine I'm selling to you"—**

[C]   **he is liable to hand over to him wine as good as the bulk of wine sold in that particular shop.**

[D]   **[If he said to him,] "These hundred jars I'm selling to you,"**

[E]   **even if it is vinegar,**

[F]   **it belongs to [the purchaser, who cannot retract]** [T. B.B. 6:9].

[G]   *[He who sells wine to his fellow, and it went sour, is not liable to make it up]* [M. 6:1K]. R. Hiyya bar Vava: "This applies in a case in which the jugs belonged to the purchaser. [The vendor] may say to him, 'I sold it to you for drinking [and you should not have kept it in your jugs for so long.]'"

[V.A]   If [one intended to designate a given jar of wine as heave offering for a larger number of jars], and he examined a jar planning to designate it as heave offering [and to drink other jugs of wine as properly tithed], he may continue to rely on that jug of wine for three days as certainly good wine.

[B] From that point onward [15c] it is subject to doubt [whether it is good wine and hence serviceable for the other jugs]. [That is, later on the wine turns out to be sour. We do not know whether wine drunk in the intervening days, between the time at which the jug was opened and its wine was found sound and the time at which the jug was rechecked and found to have turned, has been properly tithed. So, as stated here, for three days it was deemed certainly good wine, and thereafter it was subject to doubt. We now ask the meaning of this statement.]

[C] R. Simon in the name of R. Joshua b. Levi: "For the first three days it was certainly wine. For the last days it was certainly vinegar. The intervening days are subject to doubt [just as explained at B]."

[D] Said R. Abbahu, "I have heard this tradition from him [Joshua b. Levi, but I do not know] how one acts in a concrete case, for R. Yohanan has said, 'Up to three days it is certainly wine, and thereafter, it is subject to doubt.'" [Consequently, there are two conflicting views of the meaning of B.]

[E] R. La in the name of R. Eleazar, R. Yasa in the name of rabbis who go up to the schoolhouse and hear matters of advice [stated] a similar case involving a needle:

[F] "It is in accord with the following statement of R. Joshua b. Levi: 'In the case of a jug in which a smooth needle has been lost, and one came along and found it rusty—[when it is in good shape, it is subject to uncleanness, and hence assumed to be unclean, and when it is rusty, it is not subject to uncleanness at all as a useless object].'

[G] "R. Simeon in the name of R. Joshua b. Levi: '[If it is found] in the first three days [after it was lost in the jug], it is deemed certainly to have been unclean [not rusty]. If it is found in the last three days, it is deemed certainly to have been clean [rusty and useless]. The middle days are subject to doubt.'

[H] "Said R. Abbahu, 'I also heard this teaching from him, but what is there to be done [in practice], for R. Yohanan has said, 'Up to the first three days, it is certainly unclean. From that time forward, it is subject to doubt.'"

[**VI.A**]   [What follows depends upon M. Git. 3:8: *He who put aside produce so that he may designate heave offering and tithes on its account, reckoning that this produce will serve for these purposes, utilizes produce as tithed relying upon what he has designated as heave offering, in the assumption that the latter remains available. R. Judah says, "At three seasons they examine wine (to see that it remains suitable). At the time of the east wind after the Festival [of Tabernacles], when the berries first appear, and when the juice enters the unripe grapes."* Now at Y. Git. 3:8, it is further stated, "As to wine from a man's press, they designate it as heave offering and rely on it in the assumption that it remains good wine for forty days." R. Judah says, "Up to the season for the inspection of wine." It is in this context that the following discussion takes place.] R. Hiyya bar Vava asked, "If one came at the end of the week and found that the wine had turned to vinegar, is it a case in which it is clear [that the wine had turned earlier, in which case the wine treated as tithed on the basis of the present cask is now discovered not to have been tithed]? Or do we rule that only from this point onward [this keg of wine, now vinegar, no longer serves as heave offering]?" [This question is not answered.]

[**B**]   R. Isaac asked, "If the season [for examining wine] passed during the forty days [specified at A], [which takes precedence]? [Do we deem the wine to be inspected in less than forty days, since the season for inspection specified by Judah has come due? Or do we wait for the passage of the forty days?] Has the power of the inspection season nullified the effect of the forty days, or has the power of the forty days nullified the effect of the inspection season?" [This question is not answered.]

[**C**]   [With reference to M. Git. 3:8E: *At three seasons they examine wine . . .* , as cited above, A,] R. Qerispai asked, "Do they examine the wine every year, or only once every three years [at the specified seasons]?"

[**D**]   Let us derive the answer from the following: He who sells his wine, guaranteeing that it will last for a year, must make it good if it turns sour before the Festival [of Tabernacles]. [It follows that one must inspect the wine once a year.]

[**E**]   Said R. Yudan, "Interpret [the statement, D, however, in line with] the example of these Galileans, who harvest the grapes of their vineyards only after the Festival [of Tabernacles]. [It would follow from this example that the antecedent year, D, ends with the Festival. Consequently,] one may infer nothing at all [from the stated rule]."

[F]   In that case, whence shall we derive the answer to the question [at C]?

[G]   Let us derive it from the following:

[H]   *If he said it was old wine, it must be last year's. If he said it is vintage-old, it must be from the year before last* [M. 6:1/O–P].

[I]   May we then not say that it is because of a single tasting? [Hence one has to examine and taste the wine at the specified seasons, and it is on that account that one must make up the wine if it goes sour. Three full years may be subject to the guarantee. Consequently, one must inspect the wine every year, not once in three years.]

[J]   What [does he have to open and taste, if he has many such jars of wine]?

[K]   He examines a single jar [if he has many, and that suffices].

[L]   Do all of them depend upon that one jar?

[M]   Rather he examines all of the jars.

[N]   Will they not turn sour if he opens them all?

[O]   Said R. Shimi, "There are men who can feel a jar at the top and know what is inside it."

Unit **I** cites and glosses Mishnah as indicated, a significant contribution to the elucidation of Mishnah's law. Unit **II** presents an artful exercise comparing the facts of our pericope's law with those parallel, but exactly opposite, ones pertaining to the prohibition of mixed seeds. What we do not take into account is deemed consequential in the context of mixed seeds, because, in that setting, we deal with a prohibition. Hence in the commercial transaction we ignore some small volume of unwanted produce, while in the equivalent transaction involving planting seeds, we must remove produce (seed), and so throughout. The reason for the inclusion of the paired conundrum at unit **III** is clear at **III.H**, namely, the facts supplied at M turn out to be crucial to the solution of the stated problems, but, of course, the

substance of the problems is unrelated to our law. Unit **IV**
brings us back to Mishnah, citing Tosefta to complement Mishnah's discourse. The whole of unit **V** and its sequel, unit **VI**,
stand outside of the framework of Mishnah. The point of contact is merely the theme of spoiled wine.

6:2   [In Leiden MS and *editio princeps* 6:3]

[A]   *"He who sells a piece of property to his fellow for building a*
       house,

[B]   *"and so, he who contracts with his fellow to build a nuptial*
       house for his son, or a widow's manse for his daughter—

[C]   *"[the contractor] builds it four cubits by six," the words of*
       R. Aqiba.

[D]   *R. Ishmael says, "That would be little more than a cattle shed!"*

[E]   *He who wants to build a cattle shed builds it four cubits by six.*

[F]   *[If he wants to build] a small house, it is six by eight.*

[G]   *[If he wants to build] a large house, it is eight by ten.*

[H]   *[If he wants to build] a hall, it is ten by ten.*

[I]   *The height is [the sum of] half its length and half its breadth.*

[J]   *Proof of the matter is the sanctuary [1 Kings 6:17].*

[K]   *Rabban Simeon b. Gamaliel says, "Is everything [supposed to*
       be] in accord with the way in which the sanctuary is built?"

[I.A] It was taught, **[If he says, "I sell you] a centenar," he must**
       hand over to him an area twelve cubits by twelve [T. B.B.
       6:24].

[II.A] R. Hamnuna the scribe asked R. Haninah, "One verse in Scrip-
       ture says, 'It was thirty cubits high' (1 Kings 6:2), and yet an-
       other verse of Scripture states, 'It was twenty cubits high'"
       (1 Kings 6:20).

[B]   But [the latter] had heard no tradition [on this contradiction,]
       nor did he say a thing to him.

[C]   He raised the same question to R. Jeremiah.

[D]   [Jeremiah] said to him, "From the ground to the top was thirty cubits, and from the Holy of Holies in the Temple to the top was twenty cubits."

[E]   Said R. Abbahu, "He tears down the Holy of Holies! The Holy of Holies [itself] stood from the very ground to the beams, as it is written, 'He lined the walls of the house on the inside with boards of cedar; from the floor of the house to the rafters of the ceiling, he covered them on the inside with wood. . . . He built twenty cubits of the rear of the house with boards of cedar from the floor to the rafters, and he built this within as an inner sanctuary, as the most holy place' (1 Kings 6:15–16).

[F]   "Rather, from the ground upward was a space of thirty cubits. From the cherub upward was a space of twenty cubits."

[G]   Said R. Tanhuma, "There is a narrative tradition that the place of the Holy of Holies [that is, the bodies of the cherubs] does not count."

[H]   Said R. Levi, "Nor does the place of the ark count."

[I]   Said R. Levi, "And it has been taught likewise in the name of R. Judah b. R. Ilai, 'The ark stands in the middle and divides the entire space for ten cubits in all directions.'"

What is specified, M. 6:2, is the contractor's minimum obligation, first as the dispute, A–C *vs.* D, then (following Ishmael) as a set of anonymous measurements. The purchaser who requests a building for one of the stated purposes has a right to assume it will be of the specified dimensions. Unit **I** supplements Mishnah, and unit **II** pertains in general to the theme introduced by Simeon b. Gamaliel, M. 6:2K.

6:3   [In Leiden MS and *editio princeps* 6:4–6]

[A]   *He who has a cistern behind his fellow's house goes in when people usually go in and goes out when people usually go out.*

[B]   *And he may not bring his cattle in and water them from his cistern.*

[C]   *But he draws water and waters them outside.*

[D]   *This party makes himself a lock, and that party makes himself a lock.*

[E]   *He who has a vegetable patch behind the vegetable patch of his fellow goes in when people usually go in and goes out when people usually go out.*

[F]   *And he does not bring in merchants.*

[G]   *And he may not enter through it into another field.*

[H]   *And [the owner of] the outer [patch] sows seeds on the pathway.*

[I]   *[If others] have given him a path on the side with the knowledge and consent of both parties,*

[J]   *he goes in whenever he wants and goes out whenever he wants and brings merchants in with him.*

[K]   *But he may not enter through it into another field.*

[L]   *And neither one of them has the right to sow seed [on the path].*

[I.A]   [With reference to M. 6:3L: Neither one of them has the right to sow seed on the path given to the man by others,] it was taught: The owner of the outside patch may not sow seed on the path, for the other party may say to him, "I want to go in from below, [and if you sow seed on the path, I won't be able to]."

[B]   And the owner of the inner garden may not sow seed on the path, because the other party says to him, "You will spare your [garden, that is, the pathway], and then trample mine [in order to get in to your garden]."

The Talmud explains M. 6:3L's reasoning.

6:4   [In Leiden MS and *editio princeps* 6:7]

[A]   *He who had a public way passing through his field,*

[B]   *[and] who took it away and gave [the public another path] along the side,*

[C]   *what he has given he has given.*

[D]   *But what was his does not pass back to him.*

[E]   *A private way is four cubits wide.*

[F]   *A public way is sixteen cubits wide.*

[G]   *An imperial road is without limit.*

[H]   *A path to the grave is without limit.*

[I]   *A place for halting [and mourning]—*

[J]   *the judges of Sepphoris said, "It should be four qabs of space."*

[K]   *He who sells a piece of property to his fellow for making a [family] grave—*

[L]   *and so, he who receives [a piece of property] from his fellow for making a [family] grave—*

[M]   *[the contractor] makes the central space of the vault four cubits by six,*

[N]   *and he opens in it eight niches,*

[O]   *three on one side, three on the other side, and two at the end.*

[P]   *And the niches are to be four cubits long, seven cubits high, and six cubits broad.*

[Q]   *R. Simeon says, "[The contractor] makes the inside of the vault six cubits by eight,*

[R]   *"and he opens in it thirteen niches:*

[S]   *"four on one side, four on the other side, three at the end, and one at [facing] the right of the door, and one at [facing] the left of the door."*

[T]   *And [the contractor] makes a courtyard at the mouth of the vault six by six—*

[U]   *space for the bier and those who bear it.*

[V]   *And he opens in [the courtyard] two other vaults, one on one side, and one on the other.*

[W]   *R. Simeon says, "Four, in all four directions."*

[X]   *Rabban Simeon b. Gamaliel says, "All depends on the nature of the rock."*

[I.A]   [With reference to M. 6:4S: Four on one side, four on the other side, three at the end, one at the right of the door, one at the left of the door, where does the contractor make these two by the door? There is no space for them.] R. Hiyya bar Joseph said, "He makes them like door bolts. [That is, he makes the chamber like an upright bolt, placing the body in upright positions.]"

[B]   Said to him R. Yohanan, "And is it not so that even dogs are not buried in such a way?

[C]   "What does he do?

[D]   "He builds them inside as if they are on the outside. [That is, he sets them into the corner.]"

[E]   Will not those which are alongside touch them?

[F]   One will not touch the other. Those on one side will be above, and those on the other, below. [He digs the niches at different levels.]

The Talmud clarifies the specified statement of Mishnah, ignoring nearly the whole of what is before us.

7 Yerushalmi Baba Batra
Chapter Seven

7:1

[A] *He who says to his fellow, "I am selling you a kor's area of arable land"—*

[B] *[If] there were there crevices ten handbreadths deep,*

[C] *or rocks ten handbreadths high,*

[D] *they are not measured with [the area].*

[E] *[If they were] less than [the stated measurements],*

[F] *they are measured with [the area].*

[G] *And if he said to him, "Approximately a kor's area of arable land [I am selling to you],"*

[H] *even if there were there crevices more than ten handbreadths deep, or rocks more than ten handbreadths high,*

[I] *lo, they are measured with [the area].*

[I.A] [As to measuring crevices or rocks, M. 7:1E–F,] R. Yosa in the name of R. Yohanan: "But this is on condition that they form the smaller part of his field [not more than four *qabs*];

[B] "[and that they be] swallowed up in the [field, not concentrated in some one area].

[C] "And in the case of a rock which is of the measure of a quarter-*qab* in area, it is not measured with it."

[D] That [rock less than ten handbreadths] which is in the middle [of the field] is measured, that which is at the side is not measured [with the field for sale].

[E]   What is meant by the side, and what is meant by the center?

[F]   Members of the house of Yannai said, "Any area which is circumambulated by the plow is the center. Any area which is not circumambulated by the plow—this is the side."

[G]   [With reference to **I.B**, the defects in the land must be scattered about,] R. Yosé in the name of R. Yohanan came [and explained], "If the greater part of [the rock] was at one side, so that, if it should be scattered about, it would constitute the smaller part of the field, it is measured with [the field]."

[**II.**A]   [As to M. 7 : 1B, C, as to crevices ten handbreadths deep, or rocks ten handbreadths high,] how broad may they be [for that dimension has not been specified]?

[B]   R. Haggai said, "Up to four cubits."

[C]   R. Yosé b. R. Bun said, "Up to ten handbreadths."

[D]   Now if there was in the field a crevice ten handbreadths deep, but not four [broad], what is the law?

[E]   Let us derive the law from the following statement:

[F]   R. [15d] Yosa in the name of R. Yohanan said, "But this is on condition that they form the smaller part of his field, and that they be swallowed up in the field, and in the case of a rock which is a quarter-*qab* in area, it is not measured with it [= **I.A–C**].

[G]   "If it was divided in half, it is measured with it. [Therefore the measurements which are given are precise, and if the crevice was ten handbreadths deep but not four broad, it is not measured with the field as a whole when it is sold.]"

[H]   Further it is stated, "If the greater part of it was at one side, so that, if it should be scattered about, it would constitute the smaller part of the field, it is (not) measured with the field."

[**III.**A]   If there was in the field an elongated crevice, which spread over a quarter-*qab* of the field [is it measured with the field]?

[B]   R. Hiyya bar Vava asked, "If it was shaped in a crooked way [not straight], it is measured with it?

[C]   "If not, [is it not measured with it]?"

[D]   R. Yudan bar Ishmael asked, "If it was shaped like a sheet of marble, it is measured with it. If not, [is it not measured with it]?"

[E]   R. Isaac bar Tabelai asked, "If it was shaped like a throne, is it measured from the side of its seat, or from the side of its back?"

[IV.A]   R. Huna in the name of R. Hiyya in the name of R. Yohanan: "And the rule applies [to begin with] only if there is a quarter-*qab* of arable earth left [and if not, then these items in any event will not be measured within the field which has been sold]."

Units **I** and **II** directly amplify Mishnah. Unit **III** lays out a set of questions, none of them answered. Unit **IV** qualifies Mishnah.

7:2

[A]   *[If he said to him,] "A kor's area of arable land I am selling to you, as measured by a rope,"*

[B]   *[if he gave him] any less, [the purchaser] may deduct [the difference].*

[C]   *[If he gave him] any more, [the purchaser] must return [cash or additional land].*

[D]   *If he said, "Whether less or more,"*

[E]   *even if he gave him a quarter-qab's space less for a seah's area, or a quarter-qab's space more for a seah's area,*

[F]   *it belongs to [the purchaser].*

[G]   *[If it was more] than this, let him make a reckoning.*

[H]   *What does he pay back to him?*

[I]   *Cash.*

[J]   *But if he wanted, he gives him back land.*

[K]   *And why have they said, "He pays back cash"?*

[L]   *To improve the claim of the seller,*

[M]   *for if he left [in a field of a kor's space] nine qabs of space,*

[N]   *or in a vegetable patch, an area of a half-qab—*

[O]   *(in the opinion of R. Aqiba, a quarter-qab—)*

[P]   *[the buyer] will pay him back in land [and not money].*

[Q]   *And not only the quarter-qab of area alone does he return, but all the extra land.*

[I.A]   Here you say, "[If he said, 'Whether less or more, even if he gave him a quarter-*qab*'s space less for a *seah*'s area, or a quarter-*qab*'s space more for a *seah*'s area,] it belongs to the purchaser' [M. 7:2D–F]."

[B]   And there you say, "And not only the quarter-*qab* of area alone does he return, but all the extra land [M. 7:2Q]." [The supposition at A is that, under all circumstances, the quarter-*qab* remains with the purchaser, and it is only the excess over that area which is subject to the reckoning. Now in the second passage, it says that the quarter-*qab* is returned, as well as the extra land. Consequently, the two clauses appear to contradict one another.]

[C]   Thus one may say: "[M. 7:2Q applies above as well as below, so that the rule about returning the quarter-*qab* of area is to be read into M. 7:2D–F as well. The point is that] since you remove the transaction from being subject to the present rule and apply to it the measurement of the rope [= M. 7:2D–F], you return the land in accord with the measurement of the rope."

The Talmud contributes a close exegesis of Mishnah's clauses.

7:3   [In Leiden MS and *editio princeps* 7:3–4]

[A]   *"[If he said,] 'I am selling you [a kor's space of ground] measured by a rope, whether it is less or more,'*

[B]   *"[the use of the expression] less or more nullifies the reference to measuring by a rope.*

[C]   *"[If he said, 'I am selling you a kor's space of ground], more or less, measured by a rope,'*

[D]   *"[the use of the expression,] measured by a rope, nullifies the reference to less or more,"* the words of Ben Nannos.

[E]   *[If he said, "I will sell you a kor's area of ground as measured]
      by its marks and boundaries," and the difference [between the
      space thus measured and a kor] was less than a sixth, it belongs
      to [the purchaser].*

[F]   *[If it was more than] a sixth, the purchaser deducts [the dif-
      ference from the price].*

[I.A] R. Hiyya taught: **"He who sells a boy slave to his fellow, and
       the slave turns out to be a thief or swindler, he belongs to [the
       purchaser].**

[B]   **"Or if he joined a band of thugs or was under sentence of
       death from the government, lo, this is a purchase made in
       error"** [T. B.B. 4:7A–B].

[II.A] [Leiden MS and *editio princeps* place the following stich at
        Y.7:5I.A:] R. Huna said, "The excess of the sixth itself does he
        deduct." [Cf. M. 7:3F.]

        Unit **I** pursues the general theme of irrevocable transactions,
        and unit **II** lightly glosses M. 7:3F, as noted.

        7:4   [In Leiden MS and *editio princeps* 7:5]

[A]   *He who says to his fellow, "Half a field I am selling to you"—*

[B]   *they divide [the field] between them [into portions of equal
       value],*

[C]   *and [the purchaser] takes a half of his field.*

[D]   *[If he said,] "The half of it in the south I am selling to you,"*

[E]   *they divide between them [the field into portions of equal value],*

[F]   *and [the purchaser] takes the half at the south.*

[G]   *And he accepts [responsibility for providing ground for] the
       place in which the fence is to be located, and for large and small
       ditches.*

[H]   *How large is a large ditch? Six handbreadths.*

[I]   *And a small ditch. Three.*

[I.A]   It was taught: He who says to his fellow, "A half field I am selling to you, and Mr. So-and-So surrounds you[r property], and Mr. So-and-So surrounds you[r property], and half of [the field of] Mr. So-and-So surrounds you[r property], [thus specifying the borders of the field]"—[how does he give him the half field]?

[B]   R. Huna and R. Judah and R. Jeremiah—

[C]   one said, "He hands over to him a field shaped like a box."

[D]   And one said to him, "He hands over to him a field shaped like a strip."

[E]   And one said, "He hands over to him a field shaped like a ribbon."

The Talmud explains the layout of a half-field.

8 Yerushalmi Baba Batra
Chapter Eight

8:1 [In Leiden MS and *editio princeps* 8:1–2]

[A]   There are those who inherit and bequeath, there are those who
inherit but do not bequeath, bequeath but do not inherit, do not
inherit and do not bequeath.

[B]   These inherit and bequeath:

[C]   the father as to the sons, the sons as to the father; and brothers
from the same father [but a different mother], [as to one an-
other] inherit from, and bequeath to, [one another].

[D]   The man as to his mother, the man as to his wife, and the sons
of sisters inherit from, but do not bequeath to, [one another].

[E]   The woman as to her sons, the woman as to her husband, and
the brothers of the mother bequeath to, but do not inherit from
[one another].

[F]   Brothers from the same mother do not inherit from, and do not
bequeath to [one another].

[G]   The order of [the passing of an] inheritance is thus:

[H]   "If a man dies and had no son, then you shall cause his inheritance to pass to his daughter" (Num. 27:8)—

[I]   the son takes precedence over the daughter,

[J]   and all the offspring of the son take precedence over the
daughter.

[K]   The daughter takes precedence over [surviving] brothers.

[L]   The offspring of the daughter take precedence over the brothers.

[M]   The [decedent's] brothers take precedence over the father's brothers.

[N]   The offspring of the brothers take precedence over the father's brothers.

[O]   This is the governing principle:

[P]   Whoever takes precedence in inheritance—his offspring [also] take precedence.

[Q]   The father takes precedence over all [the father's] offspring [if none is a direct offspring of the deceased].

[I.A]   It is written, "If a man dies and had no sons, then you shall cause his inheritance to pass to his daughter" (Num. 27:8).

[B]   R. Ishmael taught, "Scripture has treated this particular case of inheritance differently [16a] from all other matters of inheritance which are listed in the Torah [in the same context].

[C]   "For in the case of all the others, it is written, 'And you shall give . . . ,' while in this case it is written, 'You shall cause to pass. . . .'

[D]   "It is passing from the normal course of the law for the daughter to inherit."

[E]   The sages of gentiles say, "The son and daughter are equal [when it comes to inheritance]."

[F]   For they interpret the language of Scripture as follows:

[G]   ". . . and had no son," meaning, if he indeed had a son, then the son and the daughter inherit on equal terms.

[H]   The [sages of Israel] objected, "And lo, it is written, 'And if he has no daughter, then you shall give his inheritance to his brothers' (Num. 27:9).

[I]   "Lo, if he should have a daughter, then both of them, namely, the [daughter and the brothers, by your reasoning] should inherit on equal terms [too]!

[J]   "Now you [pagan sages] concur that '. . . if he has no son' [means, then, but only then, the daughter inherits]. Here too, it means if there is no heir [then, but only then, the brothers inherit]. [Your own reasoning thus supports our reading, not yours, of the cited passages of Scripture.]"

[K]   The Sadducees [who take the same position as the pagan sages] argue as follows: "The daughter of the son and the daughter should be equivalent to one another."

[L]   For they interpret the passages as follows: "Now if the daughter of the son, who inherits on the strength of my son, will inherit me, my daughter, who inherits on the strength of direct relationship to me—is it not a matter of logic that she too should inherit me [along with the son's daughter]?"

[M]   They said to them, "No. If you have stated that the daughter of the son inherits, who does so only through a stronger claim than the brothers of the father, will you say so in the case of the daughter, who inherits solely through her standing in relationship to the deceased [grandfather]. [For you concur that, if there *are* brothers, she will not inherit a thing. That is, the granddaughter inherits where the deceased has left no sons, but she inherits over the deceased's brothers. The daughter will not inherit where the deceased has left sons. So the daughter is in a less privileged position than the granddaughter.]"

[II.A]   [How do we know that a man, as to his mother, inherits but does not bequeath? (M. 8 : 1D)] Scripture states, "And every daughter who possesses an inheritance in any tribe [of the people of Israel shall be wife to one of the family of the tribe of her father, so that every one of the people of Israel may possess the inheritance of his fathers]. [So no inheritance shall be transferred from one tribe to another]" (Num. 36 : 8–9).

[B]   And how is it possible for a daughter to receive an inheritance from two different tribes? But interpret the passage to speak of a woman whose father comes from one tribe, and whose mother from another.

[III.A]   Up to this point [we have proved from Scripture only that] the son inherits the father. What about the father's inheriting from the son [in precedence to the sons of the deceased son]?

[B]   Now if the son, who inherits only on the strength of the father, lo, he is his heir, the father, on whose strength the son stands— is it not a logical consequence that he should inherit [the son, before the other sons of the same father gain an inheritance from their deceased brother]?

[C]   [Now you may *not* then ask why the father also should not take precedence in the estate of his son over the deceased's own son, for] Scripture has said, "Relation"—meaning that a relative, namely the deceased's son, takes precedence [over the deceased's father].

[IV.A]   Up to this point we have proved only that the daughter [inherits her mother's estate]. How do we know that a son inherits his mother's estate?

[B]   Now if the daughter, who has an inferior claim on the estate of her father, has a superior claim on the estate of her mother, a son, who has a superior claim on the estate of his father, is it not logical that he should have a superior claim on the estate of his mother?

[C]   It turns out that the right of the daughter to inherit the mother's estate derives from Scripture [II.A], and the right of the son to inherit the mother's estate derives from an argument a fortiori.

[D]   Does the son take precedence over the daughter [in the estate of the mother, as he does in the estate of the father]?

[E]   R. Simeon b. Eleazar says in the name of R. Zekhariah b. Haqqaṣṣab, "So did R. Simeon b. Judah say in the name of R. Simeon, 'The son and the daughter are all the same in respect to the trib[al claim] of the mother. [They have an equal claim of inheritance on the estate of the mother].'"

[f]   R. Malokh in the name of R. Joshua b. Levi: "The law is in accord with R. Zekhariah."

[G]   R. Yannai of Cappodocia had a case [in which there was an estate involving a son and a daughter with the inheritance of their mother], and the judges were R. Huna, R. Judah b. Pazzi, and R. Aha.

[H]   Said to them R. Aha, "Our brethren abroad are mediocre, and they err in the law. Further, they rely upon the statement of R. Malokh in the name of R. Joshua b. Levi, but that statement is false.

[I]   "Thus did R. Simeon [state] in the name of R. Joshua b. Levi, 'The law is not in accord with the position of R. Zekhariah. And R. Ba, son of R. Hiyya in the name of R. Yohanan: 'The law is not in accord with the position of R. Zekhariah b. Haqqaṣṣab.'"

[J]   R. Eleazar, father of R. Isaac bar Nahman, in the name of R. Hoshaiah: "The law is not in accord with R. Zekhariah."

[K]   R. Yannai and R. Yohanan were in session. R. Yudan the Patriarch came and asked, "'And every daughter who possesses an inheritance in any tribe . . .'—what is the law [as to the son's taking precedence over the daughter (= **IV.D**)]?"

[L]   He said to him, "[The very verse you have cited proves that that is indeed the case]. The tribe of the father [and hence the right of inheritance and bequeathal] is compared to the tribe of the mother, with the consequence that, just as the father's tribe does not bequeath property to the daughter when there is a son available, so the tribe of the mother should not bequeath property to the daughter where there is a son available."

[M]   [Yudan answered,] "Or perhaps one may argue the opposite:

[N]   "Just as in the case of the tribe of the mother's bequeathing property to the daughter when the son is yet available, so the tribe of the father should bequeath property to the daughter even where there is a son to inherit the property."

[O]   Said to him R. Yohanan, "Let's get out of here. This man does not want to listen to the teachings of Torah.

[P]   "[Now how do we know that] *a man* [inherits] *his mother's estate*, and that *a man* [inherits] *his wife's estate* [M. 8:1D]?

[Q]   "Is it not the same rule for a case involving the man and his mother and the man and his wife? [We learn that a man inherits his mother from the cited verse (Num. 36:8). The Torah does not want property moved from tribe to tribe. So for the same reason that a man inherits his mother, a man will inherit his wife's estate and vice versa.]"

[V.A]   R. Isaac wanted to state the meaning of the verse and could not find it. He stated the following law:

[B]   "It is taught: 'The son . . . ,' I know only the son. As to the son of the daughter—how do I know [that he too inherits the grandfather's estate]? Scripture says, '. . . Son . . . .' [That is, a son] from any source [even from the daughter].

[C]   "'Daughter . . . ,' I know only that the daughter [inherits]. The son of the daughter, the daughter of the son, the daughter of the daughter, the son of the daughter's son—how do I know [that they inherit]?

[D]   "Scripture says, '. . . daughter . . . .' [That is, a daughter] from any source.

[E]   " 'Brothers . . . ,' I know only that brothers [inherit]. How do I know that the sons of brothers, the daughters of brothers, the sons of daughters' brothers [inherit also]?

[F]   "Scripture says, '. . . to his near relation . . . .'—under all circumstances."

Mishnah distinguishes between inheriting from a relative, and bequeathing an estate to him. The father inherits the estate of the son and bequeaths his estate to the son. The man inherits his mother's estate but does not bequeath his estate to his mother, D. The woman bequeaths her estate to her son, E, but does not inherit her son's estate, which is just what D has said. Brothers from the same mother but a different father, F, do not stand in a testamentary relationship at all, in line with C. This bare statement, of course, conceals more than it reveals, since it does not indicate, for one thing, the conditions under which a number of the testamentary relationships are to be invoked, e.g., the absence of other, closer heirs. In passing on an inheritance, if we find a son, the son gets the estate. If there is no son but there are grandsons, the grandsons take precedence over the decedent's daughter I, J. If there is no son, then, K, the daughter gets the father's estate. If there is no direct heir, then the decedent's brothers take precedence over the decedent's uncles on the father's side, M. Q adds a fresh point. If there are no direct heirs, then the decedent's father takes precedence over collateral ones, e.g., brothers and sisters of the decedent. The Talmud fairly systematically works through the Scriptural foundations for Mishnah's laws dealing with the disposition of estates. It would be difficult to improve upon the discourse before us, within the framework of the Talmud's capacity to derive its propositions through Scriptural exegesis. There is scarcely a misstep in the entire construction. Unit I is devoted to the fact that under certain circumstances the daughter may inherit the father's estate. This has two sides to it. First, we must prove that the daughter inherits at all. Second, we must show that the daughter inherits

only when there is no male heir, which is M.'s position. Unit **II**
proceeds to the parallel of the same legal anomaly, the female
line, and asks about the power of the mother to bequeath her
estate to her children. Unit **II** proves that the daughter may inherit her mother's estate; as M. 8:1E indicates that the son inherits his mother's estate, it becomes necessary to bring that fact
into alignment with the right of the daughter. After the intrusion
of unit **III**, this is what unit **IV** provides. The discussion explores the widest range of possibilities. Unit **V** then is a résumé
of proofs for a broad range of possibilities.

8:2   [In Leiden MS and *editio princeps* 8:3]

[A]   *The daughters of Zelophehad took three portions of the*
inheritance:

[B]   *the portion of their father [Num. 27:7], who was among those*
who had gone forth from Egypt, and his share along with his
brothers from the property of Hepher [their father's father], for
[Hepher] was a firstborn, receiving two portions [thereof].

[I.A]   The daughters of Zelophehad said before Moses, our rabbi, "If
we are truly the daughters of Zelophehad, let us inherit the estate of our father. If we are not the daughters of Zelophehad,
then let our mother enter into Levirate marriage [as a childless
widow]."

[B]   Forthwith: "Moses brought their case before the Lord" (Num.
27:5).

[C]   The Holy One, blessed be he, said to him, "'The daughters of
Zelophehad are right; you shall give them possession of an inheritance among their father's brethren and cause the inheritance of their father to pass to them' (Num. 27:7). Give them
real estate, give them movables, give them their father's portion,
among the brothers of their father."

[II.A]   R. Hoshaiah [not *Josiah*] said, "Among those who had gone
forth from Egypt the Land was divided up,

[B]   "for it is written, '[But the land shall be divided by lot;] according to the names of the tribes of their fathers shall they inherit'
(Num. 26:55).

[C]   "If so, why does Scripture state, 'To *these* [the land shall be divided for inheritance according to the number of names' (Num. 26:53)]?

[D]   "But it is on account of [the intent to exclude] the women and children [from the division of the Land]."

[E]   R. Yohanan said, "Among those who actually came to the Land was the Land divided up,

[F]   "for it is written, 'To these the land shall be divided [for inheritance according to the number of names]' (Num. 26:53).

[G]   "If so, why does Scripture state, '[But the land shall be divided by lot]; according to the names of the tribes of their fathers shall they inherit' (Num. 26:55)?

[H]   "The act of inheritance at hand is different from all other inheritances in the world.

[I]   "For in the case of all other inheritances in the world the living inherit the estates of the deceased, but here, the dead inherit the estates of the living. [That is, the deceased, who went forth from Egypt, are represented by their descendants. The deceased are assigned shares. This is illustrated below, X–Z]."

[J]   It was taught: R. Joshua b. Qorha says, "Among those who had come forth from Egypt and among those who were present on the plains of Moab was the Land divided.

[K]   "How so?

[L]   "He who was among those who had gone forth from Egypt and also was among those present on the plains of Moab took two portions.

[M]   "He who was among those who had gone forth from Egypt but was not present on the plains of Moab,

[N]   "and he who was present on the plains of Moab but was not among those who had gone forth from Egypt

[O]   "took a single portion."

[P]   "The daughters of Zelophehad then took five portions [*vs.* M. 8:2A]: their portion with those who had gone forth from Egypt; their portion with those who were present at the plains of Moab; the one who was firstborn took two portions; and the portion of their father among the brothers of their father."

[Q] Said R. Yosé, "The Mishnah itself does not say so [= M. 8:2A]. But: 'You shall give them a possession of an inheritance among their father's brethren and cause the inheritance of their father to pass to them' (Num. 27:7).

[R] "This is in line with that which is written: 'Thus there fell to Manasseh ten portions . . . [because the daughters of Manasseh received an inheritance along with his sons]'" (Joshua 17:5–6).

[S] [Reverting to Joshua b. Qorha's thesis:] Joshua and Caleb took three portions, their portion with those who had gone forth from Egypt, their portion with those who were present on the plains of Moab, and they also took the portion of the spies.

[T] This is in line with that which is written: "But Joshua, the son of Nun, and Caleb, the son of Jephunneh, remained alive, of those men who went to spy out the land" (Num. 14:38).

[U] But the portion of those who had complained against the Land and of the congregation of Korach fell into the common pot.

[V] And their children because of the merit of the father of their father and mother [did not die].

[W] This is in line with that which is written: "And the children of Korach did not die" (Num. 26:11).

[X] Rabbi drew a simile, [saying,] "To what is the matter to be likened? It is similar to the case of **two brothers in partnership, who went forth from Egypt. This one had nine sons, and that one had one son. They inherited an estate of ten kors. Each one of them takes a *letekh*.**

[Y] **"They returned them to their fathers who divided them up. It turned out that this one's son took half, and the sons of that one take half** [just as at **I,** above]" [T. B.B. 7:9].

[Z] R. Dosetai b. Judah drew a simile, [saying,] "To what is the matter to be likened? It is similar to the case of two brothers, priests in partnership, who were awaiting [the priestly dues] at the threshing floor. This one had nine sons, and that one had one son. They received ten *qabs* [of grain] and returned them to their fathers, who divided them. It turns out that the son of this one takes half and the sons of that one half."

[**III.**A] [To M. 8:2B: "The firstborn received two portions,"] R. Yohanan objected, "'And I will bring you into the land of your forefathers which I swore to give to Abraham, to Isaac, and to Jacob; I will give it to you for a possession' (Exod. 6:8).

[B]   "If it is spoken of as a gift, then why is it spoken of as an inheritance, and if it is spoken of as an inheritance, why is it spoken of as a gift?

[C]   "But after it was given to them as a gift, he went and gave it to them as an inheritance [thus invoking the rule of the double portion to the firstborn]."

[D]   Said R. Hoshaiah, "In any case in which the word *inheritance* is used, it is language of doubt [and Moses was in doubt]."

[E]   And they objected, "Now lo, it is written, '. . . as an inheritance for the assembly of Jacob' (Deut. 33:4). [Is this a statement of doubt]?"

[F]   He said, "There is no matter of doubt greater than this ['When Moses commanded us as a law, as an inheritance for the assembly of Jacob'], for after one labors much in the law, he finds the whole of it to be a mass of doubts."

After a brief expansion on the cited verses of Scripture, unit **I**, the division of the Land is fully explicated, unit **II**, with the three possible positions spelled out on how the division was undertaken. (Josiah must be wrong at **II.A**.) The dispute requires some secondary expansion, since **II.I** is somewhat elliptical, and the meaning of having the deceased inherit the estate of the living—that is, the living represent the dead, and the division takes place in the name of the dead—is given full instantiation at X–Z. Joshua b. Qorha's position, which intervenes, is rather excessively instantiated, that is, not only at J–O, but also at S–W. Unit **III** asks whether the Land is subject to the rules governing inheritances or gifts, **III.A–C**. The relevance, as noted, is that the inheritance involves a double portion to the firstborn. The unstated agendum here is why Moses had to address the issue to God, and Yohanan answers that question, **III.A–C**. Then Hoshaiah rejects that proposal. This is an example of the Talmud's discussing a question which is never actually asked.

8:3   [In Leiden MS and *editio princeps* 8:4]

[A]   *All the same are the son and the daughter as to matters of inheritance,*

[B]   *except that the son takes a double portion in the estate of the father [Deut. 21:17].*

[C]   *[The son] does not take a double portion in the estate of the mother.*

[D]   *The daughters are supported by the father's estate and are not supported by the mother's estate.*

[I.A]   It is written, ". . . he shall acknowledge the firstborn, by giving him a double portion of all that he has . . ." (Deut. 21:17).

[B]   How so?

[C]   [following PM:] He does not receive as an inheritance a portion of property which is to fall due to the father's estate as he does of property which is already in the full possession of the father's estate.

[D]   How so?

[E]   **If the father dies in the lifetime of the father's father, the firstborn son takes a double portion in the estate of his father, but he does not take a double portion in the estate of the father's father.**

[F]   **But if his father was a firstborn, just as he takes a portion in the estate of his father, so he takes a portion in the estate of the father of the father [T. B.B. 7:7].**

[G]   [Explaining the rule of F,] R. Simeon b. Laqish in the name of Abba bar Daliah, "The word *judgment* is used with reference to the double portion, [16b] and the word *judgment* is used with reference to the rules of inheritance.

[H]   "Just as in the matter of the rules of inheritance, you regard the son as if he were alive, to take [for the son's children] a share of the estate of his father, so with regard to the matter of the double portion, you regard the son as if he were alive too so that [the grandson, as surviving heir] takes a double portion in the estate of his father."

The Talmud explains M. 8:3B through Tosefta's expansion of it.

8 : 4   [In Leiden MS and *editio princeps* 8 : 5]

[A]   *He who says, "So-and-so, my first-born son, is not to receive a double portion,"*

[B]   *"So-and-so, my son, is not to inherit along with his brothers,"*

[C]   *has said absolutely nothing.*

[D]   *For he has made a stipulation contrary to what is written in the Torah.*

[E]   *He who divides his estate among his sons by a verbal [donation],*

[F]   *[and] gives a larger portion to one and a smaller portion to another, or treats the firstborn as equivalent to all the others—*

[G]   *his statement is valid.*

[H]   *But if he had said, "By reason of an inheritance [the aforestated arrangements are made],"*

[I]   *he has said nothing whatsoever.*

[J]   *[If] he had written, whether at the beginning, middle, or end, [that these things are handed over] as a gift, his statement is valid.*

[I.A]   R. La [in a case] divided the firstborn's portion equally among brothers.

[B]   Said to them R. Haggai, "And is it not an explicit statement of the Torah: 'He may not treat the son of the loved as the firstborn [in preference to the son of the disliked, who is the firstborn; but he shall acknowledge the firstborn, the son of the disliked, by giving him a double portion of all that he has]' (Deut. 21 : 16–17)?"

[C]   Said R. Eleazar, "By the Temple service! He most certainly can do so. For has he not got the right to do so [cf. PM]?

[D]   "If so, he may simply [give the donation] as a gift [and not under the laws of the firstborn's right to get a double portion in the inheritance]." [That is what happened at the case at I.A]

[II.A]   *If he had written, whether at the beginning, middle or end, [that the property was transmitted] as a gift, his statement is valid* [M. 8 : 4J].

[B]   Said R. Hoshaiah, "[Examples for the foregoing statement would be as follows:] 'Let my property be *given* to Mr. So-and-so as an inheritance which I have caused him to inherit. . . .'

[C]   "'Let Mr. So-and-so inherit the *gift* which I have given him. . . .'

[D]   "'Let Mr. Such-and-such inherit the inheritance which I have *given* him . . .'; [in all these cases, the use of the language of donation is adequate to remove the transaction from the laws of inheritance]."

[**II.A**]   "Write a gift over such-and-such a field, or to Mr. So-and-so. . . ." [The case is a dying man, who said, "Let all my property be given to So-and-so, and then he went and said, "Write it over and give it. . . ."]

[B]   R. Eleazar and R. Simeon b. Yaqim brought the case before R. Yohanan [for they were not sure how to decide the case]. [Was the intent to transmit ownership through the document? But a documentary donation is invalid after death.]

[C]   He [R. Yohanan] said to them, "If it was for the purpose merely of making a written note of the transaction, then write the document and hand over the property to him [since the property is not transmitted via acquisition of the document].

[D]   "But if it was to give the man ownership of the property through the written document, everyone concurs that a man does not give possession through a written document after the donor has died."

[E]   Samuel asked R. Huna, "A deed of gift in which the language used is that of a sale—what is the law?"

[F]   He said, "He has hitched [his wagon] to two wild horses [pulling in opposite directions]. [The wagon stands still. The man gains nothing.]"

[G]   [Explaining the simile just now used,] said R. Hezekiah, "They have said only: Bring two white horses and hitch them to a wagon. This one goes his way, and that one goes that way, and it turns out that the wagon will not move a step."

The simple point is that in transferring property there is a difference between inheritance and donation. If one transfers property through inheritance, he must carry out the Torah's stipulations in that regard. If he hands it over as a gift, he is free to do as he likes. Unit **I** simply shows how the distinction proposed at Mishnah works in fact, and unit **II** supplies ample exemplification for the diverse verbal formulations which will lead to the same practical conclusion. Unit **III** deals with donations and bears no relationship to Mishnah.

8:5   [In Leiden MS and *editio princeps* 8:6]

[A]   *He who says, "Mr. So-and-so will inherit me," in a case in which he has a daughter,*

[B]   *"My daughter will inherit me," in a case in which he has a son,*

[C]   *has said nothing whatsoever.*

[D]   *For he has made a stipulation contrary to what is written in the Torah.*

[E]   *R. Yohanan b. Beroqah says, "If he made such a statement concerning someone who is suitable for receiving an inheritance from him [e.g., a son among other sons], his statement is valid.*

[F]   *"But [if he made such a statement] concerning someone who is not suitable for receiving an inheritance from him, his statement is null."*

[I.A]   Said R. Yohanan, "R. Yohanan ben Beroqah's statement [M. 8:5E–F] applies only in a case in which the man spoke of one son among others or one daughter among others [cf. T. B.B. 7:18].

[B]   "But [if he spoke of] a daughter among [surviving] brothers [of the deceased], or **a brother['s inheriting the estate in place of] daughters** [T. B.B. 7:18], [it was] not [to such a case that he addressed his statement]."

[C]   Said R. Yohanan, "The law accords with the position of R. Yohanan b. Beroqah."

[D]   Rabbi asked R. Nathan bar Ba [a question].

[E]   He said, "Thus is the question:

[F]   "What is the reason of R. Yohanan b. Beroqah's ruling?"

[G]   R. Zeira said, "Thus is the question:

[H]   "Why did they say, 'The law is in accord with the position of R. Yohanan b. Beroqah?'"

[I]   [Nathan] said to [Rabbi], "Now did you yourself not teach us so: [*If the husband did not write for her, 'Male children which you have with me will inherit the proceeds of your marriage contract, in addition to their share with the other brothers,' he nonetheless is liable [to pay over the proceeds of the marriage contract to the woman's sons], for this is in all events an unstated condition imposed by the court* (M. Ket. 4:10)]? They inherit [the proceeds of the mother's marriage contract, no matter what the husband does. Here we have a case of one son among the others, and in line with what Rabbi has taught at M. Ket. 4:10, the language of inheritance is used and yet one son gets a larger share. Consequently, Rabbi must concur that the father has the power to give an inheritance to one son over others.]"

[J]   [Rabbi] said to [Nathan], "They will take [as a gift, that larger share which is coming to them]. [But as to inheritances, the law is not the same.]"

[K]   He said to him, "And even in accord with the one who said, 'They will inherit' [as specified under the laws of inheritance, not of donation], nonetheless, the power of the court suffices [to revise the law in the present case from what it is in other cases]. [Hence the cited case is not pertinent to the original question," so Rabbi replies to Nathan.]

[L]   "This is in line with that which you say there: A man does not impart ownership of his property by using the language of donation. Here he does impart ownership [in that wise].

[M]   "And similarly, A man does not impart ownership through the language of inheritance, but here he does so. [So what we have here is a special case, subject to its own logic.]"

[II.A]   There we have learned: [*If a husband wrote for his wife, "I have no right nor claim to your property, to its usufruct, to the usufruct of its usufruct, during your lifetime and after your death," he neither has the usufruct in her lifetime, nor, if she dies, does he inherit her.*] Rabban Simeon b. Gamaliel says, "If she died, he should in any event inherit her, because he has *made a stipulation against what is written in the Torah (which is that the husband inherits his wife's estate), [and whoever makes a stipulation against what is written in the Torah—his stipulation is null]"* [M. Ket. 9:1K–O].

[B]   R. Jeremiah in the name of Rab, "[The law follows Simeon in inheritances] because he has made a stipulation against that which is written in the Torah, and he who makes a stipulation against that which is written in the Torah—his stipulation is null."

[C]   This is subject to the condition that it is not a matter of monetary rights. But here [with regard to her estate] we deal with a matter of monetary rights.

[D]   What is the reason of Rab [who declares the law to accord with the position of Simeon b. Gamaliel]?

[E]   It is because it is at the end [after her death] that he acquires [the estate]. [The acquisition is through the stipulation of the court, and it is not the husband's prerogative to give up what the court stipulates in all cases.]

[F]   Said R. Yohanan, "The law is in accord with the position of Rabban Simeon b. Gamaliel."

[G]   For R. Yohanan said, "If a woman [in any circumstances] should sell or give away her property, in law what she has done should be valid.

[H]   "Why then did sages maintain that her act of sale is null?

[I]   "So that a woman should not sell her husband's property and claim, 'They are mine.' [But in the end, as Rab says, the husband does get the wife's property.]"

[J]   R. Yustini had a case before Rabbis, and they found for his antagonist. [The rabbis supported the view that the husband who nullifies his claim on his wife's estate loses out.]

[K]   He appealed to R. Simeon b. Laqish.

[L]   He said, "Go, possess what is yours [since the law follows Simeon b. Gamaliel]."

[M]   R. Jeremiah raised the question before R. Zira, "[In accord with what authority did the rabbis who decided against Yustini rule?] Rab said, 'In the end he acquires possession of them.' Said R.

Yohanan, 'The law is in accord with the position of Rabban Simeon b. Gamaliel.' R. Simeon b. Laqish said, 'Go, possess what is yours.' So *who* are these rabbis?!"

[N]   They are the rabbis vis-à-vis the case of R. Yustini!

[III.A]   ". . . and he shall inherit it . . ." (Num. 27:11). [The husband inherits his wife's estate, as a matter of Torah law, and she does not inherit his estate].

[B]   Is it possible to maintain that just as the husband inherits the wife's estate, so she inherits his?

[C]   Scripture says, ". . . it . . . ," meaning, he inherits her, she does not inherit him.

[D]   Said R. Yohanan, "In the view of sages [who differ from Simeon b. Gamaliel at M. Ket. 9:1], her father inherits her or her brother inherits her [since the husband has dealt himself out of the estate]."

[E]   R. Ba bar Mamal objected, "If you maintain that the husband inherits his wife's estate as a matter of Torah law, then he should also inherit in the case of the death of his betrothed [in the case of the death of a betrothed woman in a marriage which has not yet been consummated]."

[F]   "[The answer to this question] is in line with that which you read in Scripture: ['None of (the priests) shall defile himself for the dead among his people, except for] his nearest [of kin, . . . or his virgin sister, who is near to him because she has had no husband . . .]' (Lev. 21:1–3)—for her and not for his divorced wife or betrothed wife [whom he has not yet wed]."

[G]   [Along these same lines, he inherits] the one who is near to him, and not the one who is merely betrothed to him.

[H]   R. Hamnuna objected, "If you say that a wife does not inherit her husband as a matter of Torah law [as is the view of sages at M. Ket. 9:1],

[I]   "then the husband should inherit from the wife's estate in property which is going to come to her in the future, just as much as in property which is already subject to her ownership, [and that is not the case]."

[J]   Said R. Yosé, "Thus did Rabbi teach: 'The husband does not take a portion in property which is going to come to the wife as he does in property which is already subject to her possession.'"

[K]   Said R. Yosé b. R. Bun, "[This is no problem]. Lo, in the case of the firstborn, whose inheritance is in accord with the law of the Torah—he does not inherit in property which is going to come to him [that double portion] as he does in property which is already within the possession of the father's estate."

[L]   Said R. Isaac, "And those who write as a clause, 'The right of inheritance does not apply if there are no children in this marriage in which case the wife's property returns to the father's estate'—this is a condition regarding monetary matters, and this stipulation is valid. [Only a stipulation as to the body is invalid.]"

[M]   "And Segub was the father of Jair, who had twenty-three cities in the land of Gilead" (1 Chron. 2:22).

[N]   Now where did Jair get cities in the land of Gilead?

[O]   But he married a woman among the daughters of Manasseh, and she died, and he inherited her estate.

[P]   Now if you say that the inheritance of the wife is not a matter of Torah law, we should say, "And Segub had . . ." But it says, "And Jair had . . ." [since he inherited his wife's property].

[Q]   And along these same lines:

[R]   "And Eleazar the son of Aaron died, and they buried him at Gibeah, the town of Phinehas his son, which had been given him in the hill country of Ephraim" (Josh. 24:33).

[S]   Now how did Phinehas get property in the hill country of Ephraim?

[T]   But he married a woman among the daughters of Ephraim and he inherited her estate.

[U]   Now if you say, "The inheritance of the wife is not a matter of Torah law," then we should say, "And Eleazar had . . . ," but in fact it says, and "Phinehas had . . ."

Unit I presents a sizable exercise in unpacking the reasoning of the law. The relevance of the parallel case at M. Ket. 4:10 is excluded, and that is the net result of the discussion. Unit **II** does not relate to Mishnah, but is à propos only in the general sense of illustrating the principle that a stipulation contrary to the Torah's law is null. Unit **III** pursues the principle of Simeon b. Gamaliel that the Torah law assigns the wife's estate to her husband, and that a contrary stipulation is null.

8:6 [In Leiden MS and *editio princeps* 8:7]

[A]   *He who writes over his property to others and left out his sons—*

[B]   *what he has done is done.*

[C]   *But sages are not pleased with him.*

[D]   *Rabban Simeon b. Gamaliel says, "If his sons were not behaving properly, his memory is for a blessing."*

[I.A]   Said R. Ba bar Mamal, "*He who writes over his property to others and left out his sons—*

[B]   "concerning such a person does Scripture say, 'and whose iniquities are upon their bones . . .'" (Ezek. 32:27).

[C]   There is the following story: A man deposited his property with R. Ba bar Mamal.

[D]   He said to him, "If my children should be worthy, give them half, and take half for yourself."

[E]   His children came and took their half.

[F]   After a while they came and wanted to contend with him [for the other half].

[G]   He said to them, "Did your father not say to me only, 'If my children are worthy, give them half and take half'?

[H]   "Now since you people have behaved badly, give me back the half which I have already given to you!"

The story expands on M. 8:6A, D.

8:7   [In Leiden MS and *editio princeps* 8:8]

[A]   *He who says, "This is my son," is believed.*

[B]   *[If he said,] "This is my brother," he is not believed.*

[C]   *[The latter] shares with him in his portion [of the father's estate].*

[D]   *[If the brother whose status is in doubt] died, the property is to go back to its original source.*

[E]   *[If] he received property from some other source, his brothers are to inherit with him.*

[F]   *He who died, and a will was found tied to his thigh—*

[G]   *lo, this is nothing whatsoever.*

[H]   *[If he had delivered it and] granted possession through it to another person,*

[I]   *whether this is one of his heirs or not one of his heirs,*

[J]   *his statement is confirmed.*

[I.A]   **[If people] took for granted concerning someone that he was his son, and at the time of his death, the [putative father] said, "He is not my son,"**

[B]   **he is not believed.**

[C]   **[If] people took for granted concerning someone that he was not his son, and at the time of [the man's] death, *he said, "He is my son,"***

[D]   **he is believed** [M. 8:6A].

[E]   **[If] he was standing among tax collectors and said, "He is my son," and then he went and said, "He is my slave," he is believed.**

[F]   **[If] he said, "He is my slave," and then he went and said, "He is my son," he is not believed** [T. B.B. 7:3].

[G]   There are Tannaim who teach that he is believed.

[H]   Said R. Manna, "For instance, these people of Napta who frequently enslave their children, [and at F it may be true that he is his son]."

[I]   He who writes over his property to someone else, who was a priest,

[J]   and included were slaves,

[K]   even though the other party said, "I don't want them,"

[L]   lo, these eat heave offering.

[M]   Rabban Simeon b. Gamaliel says, "Once he has said, 'I don't want them,' the heirs [of the first party] have acquired possession of them" [T. B.B. 8:1].

[N]   Said R. La, "They differ when the matter is not subject to prior specification.

[O]   "How shall we interpret the matter?

[P]   "If it is a matter of certainty that he wants them, then all parties concur that his slaves eat food in the status of heave offering.

[Q]   "And if it is a matter of certainty that he does not want them, then all parties concur that his heirs have acquired possession of them.

[R]   "But we must interpret the dispute to apply to a case in which the matter is lacking explication, [so we do not know the facts of the matter].

[S]   "Now rabbis maintain that, at the outset, he wanted them, and now he does not want them.

[T]   "Rabban Simeon b. Gamaliel says that since he said, 'I do not want them,' the heirs have acquired possession of them."

[II.A] It was taught: Rabban Simeon b. Gamaliel says, "A will may nullify a will. [That is, if one wrote his property over to one party, then he wrote the property to some other, the latter acquires possession of the property.]

[B]   "But a gift does not nullify a gift [so in the parallel case, the first party retains possession]."

[C]   R. Abba bar Hanah, R. Yohanan, and R. Simeon b. Laqish—all three say, "In any case in which, if a person [who was dying and made a written donation] should get better and be able to retract his will, he has the right also to retract a gift which he has given."

[D]   The sister of R. Honia wrote her property to R. Honia. She fell into need and sold the property to her husband. When she had died, he came and wanted to raise the issue with him [with the deed of gift].

[E]   He said to him, "Now why did you not lay claim on me when she was alive?"

[F]   He said to him, "I did not want to bother her."

[G]   Even so, R. Ammi retrieved the property [and restored it to the husband, since she had the right to retract the gift].

A serves only to set off the contrast to B, and the focus of interest is on the explication of B at C–E. A person controls what is his, A. The brother who testifies that another man is his brother is not believed. For his testimony affects others. Thus this other party does not share in common in the father's estate. The one who gives the testimony, however, shares his part of the estate with the alleged brother, C. If the recipient should die, D, the share in the estate which the brother who gave testimony has shared goes back to his brothers. If, E, the one whose status is in doubt inherits property from some other source, all the brothers share in that property, since this one has acknowledged all of them as *his* brothers. The point of the second pericope, F–J, is clear in the contrast between F and H. If the will has not been handed over to another person, F–G, we postulate that the decedent changed his mind. If the will has been handed over to another party and assigns property to another party while the testator is still alive, the will is valid. Unit I serves M. 8:7A–E, and unit II, M. 8:7F–J. Unit I simply lays out relevant materials of T., as indicated, with light glosses. The one point of interest is at I.N–T, clear as given, namely, R. Hila's interpretation of T. Unit II goes over the ground of retracting a gift. The case, II.D–H, illustrates the position outlined in C, that is, the sister had been dying and made a written donation, then got better and retracted the donation and sold the property to her husband.

8:8   [In Leiden MS and *editio princeps* 8:9]

[A]   *"He who writes over his property to his sons has to write, 'From today and after death,'" the words of R. Judah.*

[B]   *R. Yosé says, "He does not have [to do so]."*

[C]   *He who writes over his property to his son [to take effect] after his death—*

[D]   *the father cannot sell the property, because it is written over to the son,*

[E]   *and the son cannot sell the property, because it is yet in the domain of the father.*

[F]   *[If] the father sold it, the property is sold until he dies.*

[G]   *[If] the son sold the property, the purchaser has no right whatever in the property until the father dies.*

[H]   *The father harvests the crops and gives the usufruct to anyone whom he wants.*

[I]   *And whatever he left already harvested—lo, it belongs to his heirs.*

[I.A]   R. Simeon b. Yaqim [16c] brought a problem before R. Yohanan: "[If one writes,] 'From today and after death,' his act of donation is valid, [while if one writes in a writ of divorce,] 'From today and after death,' the writ of divorce is null. [What is the difference?]"

[B]   Associates say that he answered him as follows: "That is not the proper way. [It is inconsistent that the same formula should be illegal in the case of a letter of divorce and legal in the case of a donation (Jastrow, p. 57b).]"

[C]   Said R. Yosé b. R. Bun, "He answered him as follows: 'The law governing writs of divorce is not the same as the law governing donations.'"

[D]   [Explaining what Yosé b. R. Bun has just said,] R. La stated, "In the case of a donation, if the donor wrote, 'From today it is a gift,' it is clear what purpose he served in so writing, 'After death.' Namely, his intent was to reserve for himself the usufruct [until he died, at which point the property passes into the hands of the donee].

[E]   "But in the case of a writ of divorce, if the husband wrote, 'From this day,' it is an act of cutting the relationship. Then for what purpose did this man write in the document, 'After death'? It was to reserve for himself rights to her body, [and this does not constitute a complete 'cutting off' or writ of divorce, and indeed expresses the husband's retraction of what he originally wrote]. [Consequently, the writ is nullified by his language.]"

[F]   Said R. Bun bar Kahana before R. La, "Perhaps the intent was to reserve for himself the income earned by her labor?"

[G]   He said to him, "We find no case in which a woman is married to one man [namely, the person whom she will remarry later on] while the income earned by her labor assigned to some other man [namely, her former husband]!"

[H]   R. Zira supported this position and declared him to be one of the builders of the Light [Torah].

[II.A]   [Tosefta's version] **He who says, "I made my slave, Tabi, a free man,"**

[B]   **"I made him a free man,"**

[C]   **"I am making him a free man,"**

[D]   **and, "Lo, he is a free man,"**

[E]   **"Lo, he is a free man,"—"Lo, he has made acquisition of himself—**

[F]   (R. Hiyya in the name of R. Yohanan, "On condition that there be a deed [prepared in one of these formulas].")

[G]   **"Let him be made a free man"—**

[H]   **Rabbi says, "He has made acquisition [of himself and is free]."**

[I]   **And sages say, "He has not acquired himself"** [T. B.B. 9:14].

[J]   **He who says, "I gave such-and-such a field to Mr. So-and-so,"**

[K]   **"I gave it to him,"**

[L]   **"It is given to him,"**

[M]   **"Let it be his,"**

[N]   "Lo, it is his"—

[O]   "Let Mr. So-and-so take part of my possessions,"

[R]   "It is to be handed over to him as a gift"—

[S]   Rabbi says, "He has made acquisition of it."

[T]   And sages say, "He has not made acquisition of it."

[U]   "But they force the heirs to carry out the statement of the decedent" [T. B.B. 9:13].

[V]   It was taught: **Rabban Simeon b. Gamaliel says, "He who writes *diatimon* [a will] in a foreign language—lo, this has the status of a gift"** [T. B.B. 9:14I].

[W]   R. Hanin in the name of R. Joshua b. Levi: "I have called upon all those who are masters of languages to find out the meaning of *diatimon*, and no one said a thing to me about it."

[X]   **He who says, "Let my property be given to So-and-so. If he should die, then to Such-and-such. If he should die, then to Such-and-so"—**

[Y]   **the first-named takes precedence.**

[Z]   **If the second-named should die in the lifetime of the first, the first enjoys the usufruct, and when he dies, the property goes back to the heirs of the donor.**

[AA]   **If the third-named should die in the lifetime of the second, the first-named enjoys the usufruct, and when he dies, the property is returned to the heirs of the donor.**

[BB]   **If the second-named and the third-named should die in the lifetime of the first, the first enjoys the usufruct, "and he acquires ownership of the real estate [which he has the right to sell]," the words of Rabbi.**

[CC]   **Rabban Simeon b. Gamaliel says, "The first has the right to the usufruct alone** [T. B.B. 8:4] [but he may not sell the land]."

[DD]   Hezekiah said, "The law is in accord with Rabbi."

[EE]   Said R. Yannai, "Rabbi concurs that [the first] does not give over this property under the law of gifts in contemplation of death. [That is, even though Rabbi says the first party may sell the land, he concurs that he cannot give the land away under the provisions of the law of gifts in contemplation of death. Why not? The property under that law passes after death. But at the point at which the man dies, the second party in the line of succession already has acquired ownership of the land. Accordingly, in this instance the law of gifts in contemplation of death is null, having been set aside by the special circumstances of the original donation.]"

[FF]   Said R. Yohanan, "Nor does it fall into the category of the gift of a healthy person. [The man cannot give away the property either. The original donor gave him the property for his benefit, and not for the purposes of transfer to a third party.]"

[GG]   That is in line with the following case:

[HH]   A woman deeded her property as a gift to a certain person. She fell into need and sold her property to her husband. R. Hiyya bar Madaya brought the case before R. Yosé [with the following argument]: "Did not R. Yannai say, 'Rabbi concurs that the first does not give over this property under the law of gifts in contemplation of death'? [That is, the woman was in the status of the first of the sequence of recipients. In Rabbi's view, such a person has the right to ownership of the property itself, and, consequently, just as, if the man should sell the property, it is a valid sale, so here too, if the woman disposed of the property, it is valid.]"

[II]   [Yosé] said to [Hiyya], "R. Yohanan [holds] that it also does not fall into the category of the gift of a healthy person [so the woman cannot dispose of the property in any wise but must keep it and derive benefit from it throughout her lifetime]. [Consequently, she cannot dispose of it at all through a donation. Her gift of the property was null.]

[JJ]   "In the case of this woman, since her husband was liable to provide her maintenance, her deed does not fall into the category of the gift in contemplation of death. [During her lifetime she cannot dispose of the property, since it is indentured to the husband. She cannot sell it for her own needs, since the husband provides for her. Hence any disposition of the land falls after death, at which point the husband takes precedence over someone to whom she might have proposed to give or sell the land. The prior transaction was null.]"

[KK]   Up to this point we have assumed that the husband was providing for her, as he was liable to do, bread and legumes. But is he
obligated if she wanted chicken! [If then she should want what
the husband is not obligated to provide, she *may* then sell the
property for her own benefit, and the foregoing argument does
not pertain.]

[LL]   This is in line with that which we have learned: The first party
enjoys the usufruct and may purchase real estate, [that is, with
the usufruct; the first party may use the proceeds for whatever
he needs]. [Here too, the woman may do so.]

[MM]   That is to say, She may then sell the real estate and buy herself a
burial plot [so she may indeed make use of the property and
usufruct in any way she likes].

[NN]   Said R. Yosé, "And those who write [in a marriage contract] a
clause to provide even for most expensive foods [write in a valid
clause, which is enforceable]."

[OO]   Said R. Jacob b. Aha, "It is taught there: A burial plot is in the
status of appropriate maintenance. As you say there, one may
sell the land to buy food, so here, one may sell the land to buy a
burial place." [Cf. PM for the reading translated here.]

[PP]   Said R. Yosé, "And those who write as a clause, 'The right of
inheritance does not apply if there are no children in this marriage' [in which case the wife's property returns to the father's
estate]—this is a condition regarding property, and this stipulation is valid." [Cf. 8:5 **IV.**L reproduced here, following PM].

Unit **I** compares the documentation and language for a donation
with that serving a writ of divorce, for reasons clear in the Talmud itself. The discussion is complete and fully articulated.
Unit **II** is built out of Tosefta and the amplification of Tosefta.
Its point of contact with Mishnah would appear to be the same
general problem, namely, gifts during lifetime to take effect after
death. That surely accounts for **II.**X–CC, the component of
Tosefta subjected to sustained analysis. The earlier materials pre-
sumably have been inserted whole, because of the interest in the
consequential passage. If that is not the reason for the inclusion
of **II.**A–W, then I do not know why this mass of statements is
here. The discussion of X–CC+DD is fully annotated and re-

quires no further comment. The better text for LL–PP is presented at Y. Ket. 9:1. I have followed PM's preferences here.

8:9   [In Leiden MS and *editio princeps* 8:10]

[A]   *[If] he left adult and minor sons, the adults may not take care of themselves [from the estate] at the expense of the minor sons,*

[B]   *nor may the minor sons support themselves [out of the estate] at the expense of the adult sons.*

[C]   *But they divide the estate equally.*

[D]   *If the adult sons got married [at the expense of the estate], the minor sons [in due course] may marry [at the expense of the estate].*

[E]   *But if the minor sons said, "Lo, we are going to get married just as you did [while father was still alive]"—*

[F]   *they pay no heed to them.*

[G]   *But what the father [while alive] gave to them he has given.*

[H]   *[If] he left adult and minor daughters, the adults may not take care of themselves [from the estate] at the expense of the minor daughters,*

[I]   *nor may the minors support themselves [from the estate] at the expense of the adult daughters.*

[J]   *But they divide the estate equally.*

[K]   *If the adult daughters got married [at the expense of the estate], the minor daughters may get married [at the expense of the estate].*

[L]   *And if the minor daughters said, "Lo, we are going to get married just as you got married [while father was still alive],"*

[M]   *they pay no heed to them.*

[N]   *This rule is stricter in regard to daughters than in regard to sons.*

[O]   *For the daughters are supported at the disadvantage of the sons*

[M. 9:1], but they are not supported at the disadvantage of [other] daughters.

[I.A]   R. Jeremiah asked the following question before R. Zira: "If the older ones took a hundred jugs of wine, worth twenty *denars*, do the minors take a hundred jugs of wine, worth [only] ten *denars*?"

[B]   He said to him, "Just as these have taken [wine of a given value], so the others take [wine of a given value]."

The Talmud's clarification of Mishnah is obvious. We take account of the value of what is divided, not merely the volume.

9 Yerushalmi Baba Batra Chapter Nine

9:1

[A] *He who died and left sons and daughters—*

[B] *when the estate is large, the sons inherit, and the daughters are supported [by the estate].*

[C] *[If] the estate is small, the daughters are supported, and sons go begging at [peoples'] doors.*

[D] *Admon says, "Merely because I am male, do I have to lose out?"*

[E] *Said Rabban Gamaliel, "I concur in the opinion of Admon."*

[I.A] [16d] Thus is the meaning of the Mishnah: *The daughters are supported* [for their needs for food, but not clothing, a dowry, and the like], *and the sons go begging at peoples' doors* [M. 9:1C].

[B] R. Jeremiah in the name of Rab: "[The rule of M. 9:1B is invoked] when there are ample resources for maintaining [both sons and daughters] for twelve months."

[C] Samuel said, "That [view, that maintenance is for twelve months,] is the opinion of Rabban Gamaliel bar Rabbi. But sages say, '[The estate is deemed sufficient only if it can support the children] until they reach maturity or until they are married.'"

[D] And there is in this ruling a lenient side [for the other heirs to the estate], and there also is a strict side.

[E]   Sometimes they may be near the age of maturity [which is to the advantage of the other heirs], and sometimes they may be distant from the age of maturity.

[F]   They asked before R. Hiyya bar Vava, "What tradition from R. Yohanan do you have?"

[G]   He said to them, "I have no tradition whatever from him in this matter, except for that which Nathan bar Hoshaiah raised before R. Yohanan: 'If there was available adequate food for these and for those for twelve months, and the property diminished in value [so that the estate turns out to be unable to support them, as originally estimated], [what is the law]?'

[H]   "He said to him, 'Since they began [receiving support from the estate] with permission, they have begun [and continue to receive such support as the estate can provide through the remaining period, even if it is less than the full twelve months].'"

[I]   [What is the law if the estate was estimated to be incapable of supporting the heirs for a year and then increased in value and turned out to be suitable for that purpose?] R. Haninah and R. Mana—

[J]   one of them said, "And the rule [that the children are supported] applies only if there is sufficient [value in the estate from beginning to] end [to maintain them] for twelve months."

[K]   And the other said, "Even if at the outset there is not sufficient value in the estate to support both these and those for twelve months, but the estate grew in value so that there is sufficient value to maintain these and those for twelve months, the estate does indeed support them."

[L]   [R. Hisda asked, "If there was not available sufficient food for twelve months, but the property rose in value, what is the law?"] Said R. Ami, "The Babylonians derive the answer from the following:

[M]   "'If the heirs went and sold [off part of the estate], they have sold off what belongs to them [so the property of the estate is deemed to belong to them].'

[N]   "All the more so if the estate should be greater in value [than what is needed for the support of the orphans for twelve months], should they divide up [what is in excess of what is required]."

[O]   [Following PM:] If there were insufficient resources for the estate for maintaining the orphans for twelve months, what is the law as to the sons saying to the daughters, "Take what is coming to you and go forth"? [Can the sons tell them that they will buy out their share in the estate, and the daughters must then leave the property?]

[P]   Said R. Abedomi, "Let us derive the answer from the following: [He who was married to two wives, who died, and afterward he died, and the orphans claim the marriage settlement owing to their mother's estate, and there are there funds to pay for only two marriage settlements—they divide the estate equally. If there was there an excess of a single denar over the necessary funds, these collect the marriage settlement owing to their mother's estate, and those collect the marriage settlement owing to their mother's estate.] If [the orphans] said, "We reckon the value of the estate of our father at one denar more" so that they may collect the marriage settlement owing to their mother, they do not listen to them, but they make an estimate of the value of the property in court (M. Ket. 10:2). [Here too they do not allow the male heirs to buy out the interest of the female heirs. A court assesses the worth of the estate, and if the estate will not support the heirs for twelve months, the entire estate goes to the female heirs.]"

[Q]   R. Hisda raised the question: "If there was sufficient food for these and those for twelve months, but, in addition, there was a widow to support, what is the law [as to the widow's diminishing the estimated resources of the estate]?

[R]   "Now is this rule, which you have stated, that the estate be sufficient to support these and those for twelve months, reckoned in addition to the obligation of paying off the marriage contract of the widow, in addition to the support of the daughters, in addition to paying off a debt secured by a deed, in addition to paying off a debt before witnesses, and in addition to the costs of burial?"

[S]   The widow and the daughters are equivalent to one another; the widow and the sons are equivalent to one another. [Each is supported at the estate's expense.]

[T]　The claim of the widow does not override the claims of the daughters, and the claim of the daughters does not override the claim of the widow. [This then has answered Q–R.]

[U]　There are cases in which the claim of the widow does override the claim of the daughters as well as the sons. [Her claim is prior, and she collects what is owing, with the result that the estate is diminished so the male and female heirs receive less.]

[V]　Just as the widow's claim overrides the claim of the daughters as well as the sons, so will the widow's claim not override the claim of the sons [alone, even when there are no daughters to support]?

[W]　The reason [that she cannot lay claim to override the claim of the sons] is that she is able to lay claim to her marriage settlement and thereby to cause the loss of her claim of support. [That is, if she receives her marriage settlement, then she does not have a claim for further support from the estate. So her claim for support is limited. But there is a widow, male heirs, and female heirs, since, to begin with, the daughters are supported by the estate only by reason of a remedy supplied by sages, when the widow claims her marriage settlement, it is with that same authority, namely, the sages. The sons' right to inherit is secured by the higher authority of the Torah (PM).]

[X]　This is in line with the following [which shows that a claim for settlement of the marriage contract ends the right of support]:

[Y]　The widow of R. Shobetai was wasting the assets of the estate [by spending too much on her own maintenance]. The children came and approached R. Eleazar. He said to them, "What can we do for you? You are a foolish people, [you have no remedy against her]."

[Z]　When they went out, they said, "As to her marriage settlement, what should we do?"

[AA]　Someone told them, "Pretend to sell some of the estate's property, and she will come and lay claim for her marriage settlement, on account of which she will lose the claim of support from the estate."

[BB]　After some days she came and approached R. Eleazar. He said to her, "May a curse come upon me, if I said a thing to them."

[CC]   [He said,] "Now what can I do for you, and it is a blow of deceivers [Pharisees] which has struck you."

[II.A]   R. Hananel in the name of R. Zeira in the name of Abba bar Jeremiah: "Two rulings did Hanan lay down, and the law is in accord with his opinion.

[B]   "Seven rulings did Admon lay down, and the law is not in accord with his opinion."

[C]   R. Ba bar Zabeda in the name of R. Isaac b. Haqulah, "In every place at which we have learned, 'Said Rabban Gamaliel, I concur in the opinion of Admon,' the law in fact is in accord with Admon."

Unit **I** presents a protracted inquiry into the matter of an estate's having sufficient resources to support the minor heirs. After clarifying some basic facts, the Talmud proceeds to raise acute analytical issues. As the discussion proceeds, it moves somewhat far from the original question, but each step in the process is logically an extension of the preceding. Unit **II** provides some facts relevant to M. 9:1D's Admon, and belongs at the fuller discussion of the materials of Admon and Hanan at M. Ket. 13:1ff. The remainder of the discussion at 9:1 belongs with M. 9:2, and I have moved it to that pericope.

9:2   [In Leiden MS and *editio princeps* 9:2–3]

[A]   *[If] he left sons and daughters and one whose sexual traits were not clearly defined,*

[B]   *when the estate is large, the males push him over onto the females.*

[C]   *[If] the estate is small, the females push him over onto the males.*

[D]   *He who says, "If my wife bears a male, he will get a maneh,"*—

[E]   *[if] she bore a male, he gets a maneh.*

[F]   *[If he said, "If she bears] a female, [she will get] two hundred zuz,"*

[G]   *[if] she bore a female, she gets two hundred zuz.*

[H]   *[If he said, "If she bears] a male, [he will get] a maneh, if [she bears] a female, [she will get] two hundred zuz,"*

[I]   *if she bore a male and a female, the male gets a maneh, and the female gets two hundred zuz.*

[J]   *[If] she bore a child whose sexual traits were not clearly defined, he gets nothing.*

[K]   *If he said, "Whatever my wife bears will get [a maneh]," lo, this one gets [a maneh].*

[L]   *And if there is no heir but that [child lacking defined sexual traits], he inherits the entire estate.*

[I.A]   [Tosefta's version] It was taught: **He who says, "He who informs me that my wife has given birth to a male gets two hundred, [or if she gave birth] to a female, he gets a maneh"**—

[B]   **[if] she gave birth to a male, [the messenger] gets two hundred.**

[C]   **[If she gave birth to] a female, he gets a maneh.**

[D]   **[If she gave birth to] a male and a female, the messenger gets only a maneh** [T. B.B. 9:5].

[E]   Said R. Mana, "The anguish of the news about the daughter nullifies the joy of the news about the son."

[II.A]   Samuel said, "They impute ownership to a fetus."

[B]   R. Eleazar said, "They do not impute ownership to a fetus."

[C]   The following teaching is at variance with the opinion of R. Eleazar:

[D]   A proselyte who died, and the property of whom Israelites plundered [in the assumption that he had no legal heir], and it became known that he had a son, or that his wife was pregnant—all of them are liable to return the property [so the fetus inherits].

[E]   If they returned the property, and afterward the son died, or his wife aborted, he who holds the property at the last has acquired rightful ownership of it.

[F]   Does he who had ownership at the outset acquire rightful ownership or not? [This fetus, after all, died.]

[G]   Interpret the matter as his having given up the right of ownership by reason of despair. [That is, the one who held the property at the outset took for granted he would not then get it back, because of the fetus; so he gave up his right to it.]

[H]   And even in accord with Samuel he does not differ in this case [which differs from his statement above, for the reason stated at G].

[I]   Or perhaps even at the end, one should not acquire rightful possession any longer because of his despairing [of retaining ownership of the property of the proselyte, since he does not know whether or not there has been a viable heir]? [This objection is not answered.]

Unit **I** supplements Mishnah. Unit **II** then utilizes Mishnah to investigate a separate, but intersecting, question, namely, assigning ownership of property to a fetus, for this is what the father does at M. 9:2. But the whole of unit **II** is essentially distinct from Mishnah before us. The discussion here is abbreviated; the full version at Y. Yeb. 4:1 should be consulted.

9:3   [In Leiden MS and *editio princeps* 9:4–5]

[A]   *[If] he left adult and minor sons—*

[B]   *[if] the adults improved the value of the estate,*

[C]   *the increase in value is in the middle [shared by all heirs].*

[D]   *If they had said, "See what father has left us. Lo, we are going to work it and [from that] we shall enjoy the usufruct,"*

[E]   *the increase in value is theirs.*

[F]   *And so in the case of a woman who improved the value of the estate—*

[G]   *the increase in value is in the middle.*

[H]   *If she had said, "See what my husband has left me! Lo, I am going to work and enjoy the usufruct,"*

[I]   *the increase in value is hers.*

[I.A]   Said R. La, "[That (M. 9:3D) is the case only] if they made their statement before a court."

[B]   Members of the house of R. Yannai said, "Even [if the adult heirs added] a clay utensil [to the estate, the minors have a share in it.]" [Cf. Jastrow, p. 1076b.]

[C]   Rab said, "Even [if they contributed] a basket, even a spade [the minors enjoy their share therein]."

[D]   R. Hiyya taught, "Even a needle, even a tightly sealed jar."

[II.A]   Said R. Haninah, "He who marries off his son in a house—[the son] has acquired possession of the house."

[B]   R. Hoshaiah taught, "[He has acquired possession of the house] but not the movables therein."

[C]   R. La divided the hall between himself and his son.

[D]   R. Haggai raised the following question of R. Yosé: "If the bridal chamber was in the bedroom [of his father's house], and [the father] made the wedding meal for him in the dining room, what is the law [as to the son's acquiring ownership of the whole area]?"

[E]   He said to him, "Will [the son] not see the father and throw him out? [The location of the bridal chamber is the main thing, and that is what the son gets.]"

[III.A]   R. Joshua b. Levi said, "They divide up [the estate] for the minor [heirs] in behalf of the adults [who wish to be separate]. But [the question is], [17a] [if] the minors went and found something of greater value [which the adults had gotten], and then objected [to the division], [what is the law]?"

[B]   R. Abbahu said, "[The adults] take an oath [to the minors that there was nothing of value beyond what had been divided]."

[C]   Said R. Mana, "Whoever lays claim against his fellow bears the burden of proof, except in this case."

[D]   R. Hiyya the Great said, "In general, brothers are regarded as partners down into the third generation [unless there is a court action as at M. 9 : 3].''

[E]   Said R. Rabbah bar Abun, ''So did R. Hamnuna teach.''

[IV.A] Said R. Ammi, ''A son who was observed [to do business] on his own during the father's lifetime—what he has acquired he has acquired for himself [and not for the father's estate, after death].''

[B]   This is in line with the following case:

[C]   A man became a scribe [at the expense of the father, who had paid the tuition for his studies]. His brothers wanted to divide [his salary with him]. The case came before R. Ammi. He said, ''Thus do we rule: 'A person who found an object—do his brothers share it with him?' [Obviously not.]''

[D]   A man went out on a mission [for a salary]. His brothers wanted to divide [his salary] with him. The case came before R. Ammi. He said, ''Thus do we rule: 'A man who went out and made his living as a bandit—do his brothers share [his booty] with him?'''

[E]   R. Horaina, brother of R. Samuel bar Suseretai—his brother wanted to divide up [what each party was making, that is, form a common pot of their earnings or profits]. He said to him, ''Alexander, my brother, you know that our father left us two thousand. [You yourself know what father left us. There were only two thousand of his. Whatever there is in addition is what I myself earned when father was alive, and it is mine, not part of the estate.]''

[V.A]   *And so in the case of a woman* [M. 9 : 3F–I].

[B]   Said R. La, ''[That is the case only if] she made that statement before a court.''

Unit I lightly glosses Mishnah, as indicated. I do not know why unit II is included. Perhaps it serves to indicate that the father may assign property to his heirs while he is yet alive, and, after he dies, the other heirs have no claim on the property. But that is a remote connection indeed to what is actually under discussion. Unit III raises a secondary question about minors' rejection of the evaluation of the estate for which Mishnah provides. Unit

IV, finally, places firm limits on the obligation of the adults to contribute their personal earnings to the estate.

9:4   [In Leiden MS and *editio princeps* 9:6]

[A]   *Brothers who were joint holders [in an inherited estate], one of whom fell into public office—*

[B]   *[the charge or benefit] fell to the common fund.*

[C]   *[If] he became ill and was healed, the healing is at his own expense.*

[D]   *Brothers, some of whom made presents as groomsmen [at their father's expense] while their father was alive,*

[E]   *[and after the father's death] the groomsmen's gift returned to them [when they got married]—*

[F]   *it has returned to the common fund.*

[G]   *For the groomsmen's gift [is deemed a loan and] is recoverable in court.*

[H]   *But he who sends his fellow jugs of wine and oil [in his father's lifetime]—*

[I]   *they are not recoverable in court,*

[J]   *because they count as a charitable deed.*

[I.A]   [Tosefta's version] **Brothers, one of whom was appointed royal commissioner—**

[B]   **if it was on account of his ownership of property held in common that he fell into this office,**

[C]   **they collect [the losses of the office] from the common fund.**

[D]   **But if it was on his own account that he fell,**

[E]   **they collect [the losses of the office] from the householder himself [M. 9:4A–B, T. B.B. 10:5].**

[F]   This is in line with the following:

[G]   R. Nahman bar Samuel bar Nahman was drafted for service on the council (*boulé*) [and wished to charge the heavy expenses to the common estate]. The case came before R. Ami. He ruled, "If it was because of the property of Nahman that he has been drafted, then let it be paid out for him from his own property. And if not, let it be paid out from the common fund."

[II.A] If he fell ill and was healed, the healing is at the expense of the common fund [cf. M. 9:4C].

[B] It was taught: **Rabban Simeon b. Gamaliel says, "In the case of any ailment involving medical care at fixed cost—she is healed at the expense of her marriage settlement. But as to [ongoing] medical care of unlimited cost—lo, that is equivalent to any other aspect of her [everyday] support [and the husband pays]** [T. Ket. 4.5I].

[C] This is in line with the following:

[D] A relative of R. Simeon bar Vava had eye trouble. She came before R. Yohanan [to claim support from her husband]. He said to her, "Has your physician set a fixed price for his treatment? If he has set a fixed price, then the cost comes from your dowry. If he has not set a fixed price for the treatment, then your husband must pay for the cost of the treatment."

[E] [Yohanan has thus shown the alternatives to the plaintiff, thus hinting to her as to an appropriate answer. This is poor judicial practice,] for have we not learned, "Do not behave like advocates"?

[F] And [note] that which R. Haggai in the name of R. Joshua b. Levi [said], "It is forbidden to reveal one's decision to an individual, [surely he should not have told her what he did]."

[G] [In reply] one may say: R. Yohanan knew that she was an honest woman, on which account he told her [what choices lay before him as judge].

[H] [Furthermore,] if the woman's husband claimed that the physician had stipulated a fixed fee for his services, and she claimed that the physician had not done so, to which party do we listen? Is it not to the husband [who can stipulate a fixed fee anyhow]?

[I] Said R. Mattenaiah, "That which you have said [at F] applies to him whom the judgment will not favor. But as to him whom the judgment will favor, one may inform him of the matter."

If the estate is not divided, M. 9:4A–B, what affects one partner in matters of public service affects all, for good or ill, A–B.
But if there is illness, the common fund is not used for the medical expense. D–G and H–J are explained in the contrast of G
and J. The groomsman gives a gift which is reciprocated when
he is married. G then explains its status. Unit I then cites a pertinent passage of Tosefta, to which it appends a precedent. Unit
II moves on to the matter of M. 9:4C, healing from the common
fund, but, as we see, the discussion is based on the materials of
M. Ket. 4:9, and the real issue is the conduct of the judge in
the cited case.

9:5   [In Leiden MS and *editio princeps* 9:7]

[A]   *He who sends gifts to his father-in-law's household—*

[B]   *[if] he sent gifts worth a hundred manehs and consumed a wedding feast of even a denar—*

[C]   *[if he divorced his wife, the gifts] are not recoverable.*

[D]   *[If he did not eat a wedding feast at all,] lo, they are recoverable.*

[E]   *[If the husband] had sent many gifts, which were to be returned
with her to her husband's house, lo, they are recoverable.*

[F]   *[If he had sent] few gifts, which she was to use while in her
father's house, they are not recoverable.*

[I.A]   Someone sent to his betrothed substantial gifts. His relatives
said to him, "Don't you eat a thing there." He went and paid no
heed to them and ate. Then the house fell down, and [the relatives of the betrothed] acquired possession of the whole [of the
gift which he had sent].

[B]   Someone sent to his betrothed twenty-four wagonloads of various kinds of leek plants between Passover and Pentecost.

[C]   And what troubled the rabbis was only where he had gotten the
seed for flax and olives.

[II.A]   R. Perida paid his respects to R. Judah the Patriarch by sending
him two kinds of radishes between the New Year and the Fast.
Now it was at the end of the Sabbatical Year, and [radishes were

so abundant] that one could taste in them [the flavor of the scent deriving from their having been carried by a camel].

[B]   Rabbi said to him, "Are they not still forbidden [as produce of the Seventh Year]? Are they not the stubble of the field [growing in that year, which may not be eaten]?"

[C]   He said to him, "At the end of the Sabbatical Year were they sown."

[D]   Forthwith Rabbi permitted purchasing produce immediately at the end of the Sabbatical Year [without waiting until the crops of the year following the Sabbatical Year had begun to appear on the market].

Unit **I** deals with our pericope of Mishnah and shows what is at issue in keeping the law. The rest of the materials pertain to gift-giving in general and bear no relation to our law.

9:6   [In Leiden MS and *editio princeps* 9:8]

[A]   *A dying man who wrote over his property to others [as a gift but] left himself a piece of land of any size whatever—*

[B]   *his gift is valid.*

[C]   *[If] he did not leave himself a piece of land of any size whatever,*

[D]   *his gift is not valid.*

[E]   *[If] he did not write [in the deed of gift], "who lies dying,"*

[F]   *[and if, after recovery, he wishes to reclaim his property, so] he says he had been dying,*

[G]   *and [the recipients] say, "He had been healthy"—*

[H]   *"he has to bring proof that he had been dying," the words of R. Meir.*

[I]   *And sages say, "He who lays claim against his fellow bears the burden of proof [and the recipient must prove that the donor had been healthy]."*

[I.A]   R. Jeremiah in the name of Rab: "[If] he left himself movables, he has done nothing whatsoever.

[B]   "But if he left himself ready cash and purchased real estate with it, it is as if he left himself a piece of real estate."

[C]   As to that which you say, *If he left himself a piece of land of any size whatever, his gift is valid*—even if he did not recover.

[D]   *If he did not leave himself a piece of land of any size whatever, his gift is not valid*—even if he recovered.

[E]   This [fact, that if the man was dying, the property is transferred under the stated condition] is in line with that which R. Yohanan said in the name of R. Yannai: "They have treated the verbal declaration of a dying man as equivalent in force to the deed of a healthy man who wrote a deed of gift and handed over the property, [in that, in the former case, a formal act of acquisition is not required for ownership to be deemed to have been transferred]."

[F]   [Now that rule applies] if the man died from the very disease from which he was suffering [when he made his statement]. [But if he got better, then the statement is not one of a dying man, and the rule cannot be invoked.]

[G]   Someone who suddenly fell sick, who divided his estate, whether on an ordinary day or on the Sabbath—what he has done is confirmed.

[H]   But if he was a healthy person, [his statements are null] until he writes in the deed, "[for transfer] through money, deed, or usucaption."

[II.A]   [We now consider a case parallel to the one at M. 9:6 E–I, namely, whether we decide a case by reference to the facts now prevailing, or to those prevailing at the time of the event. The issue is the resolution of doubt, with special reference to an area the status of which changes. We know that a case of doubt involving uncleanness affecting public domain is resolved in a lenient way, and we assume that cleanness prevails. A case of doubt involving uncleanness affecting private domain is resolved in a strict way, and we assume that uncleanness prevails. There is a domain which at one season is deemed to fall into public domain, at the other, private domain, namely, a valley, which in the dry season—when people walk there—is held to be public domain, and in the rainy season, private. The relevance of this problem to the present case will be clear in a moment.] Said R. Yohanan, "[If] there was a case of uncleanness as a matter of doubt affecting a valley—

[B]   "whether this took place in the dry season or the rainy season—

[C]   "there is a dispute between R. Meir and sages.

[D]   "[The dispute works as follows:] [if] one comes to inquire [of a sage as to the disposition of the case] in the dry season, they receive the inquiry in accord with the rule prevailing at the dry season. If it is in the rainy season, they receive the inquiry in accord with the rule prevailing at the rainy season. [This then would accord with Meir's view at M. 9:6H, since the man is now healthy and has to prove the situation prevailing earlier was different from that prevailing now. The sages' view is readily reconstructed.]"

[E]   Said R. Yohanan, "But that is on the condition that [the question on the rainy season is brought] on days near the rainy season [and not many months later]."

[III.A]   R. Yannai in the name of Rab: "The claim of the one who has a deed [which requires interpretation] is subordinated, [and the language of the deed is interpreted in favor of the claim of the defendant]."

[B]   Said to him R. Yohanan, "And does not the Mishnah make this same point: *If he did not write in the deed of gift, 'who lies dying, and he says that he had been dying . . .'* [M. 9:6E–F]?"

[C]   R. Yannai then praised [R. Yohanan, for proving that his position is supported by M.]: "'Those who lavish gold from the purse' (Isa. 46:6). 'My son, keep sound wisdom and discretion; let them not escape from your sight'" (Prov. 3:21).

[D]   A youth sold his property, and the case came before R. Hiyya bar Joseph and R. Yohanan, [since the relatives claimed that he sold the property as a minor and had no power to do so].

[E]   R. Hiyya bar Joseph ruled, "The prevailing supposition is that [the witnesses signed the deed] for a person of mature mind, [and the purchaser of the property has the advantage]."

[F]   R. Yohanan ruled, "Since [the purchaser] has come to remove property from the family, it is his burden to bring proof [that the youth was of mature capacities when he made the sale of his property]."

[G]   Says R. Yohanan, "[In general] the claim of the one who has a deed is superior." [This is explained presently, since it contradicts A–B, above.]

[H]   R. Yosa asked before R. Yohanan, "Now what [is to be done, if that is the case, with the following] statement of Rab(bi), for Rab(bi) said, 'The claim of the one who holds the deed is subordinated.'"

[I]   He said to him, "It is the opinion of all parties that the claim of the one who holds a deed is superior."

[J]   "Now how can you say so? [For we have just made the following statement:] The case came before R. Hiyya bar Joseph, who ruled, 'The prevailing supposition is that the witnesses signed the deed for a person of mature mind, and the purchaser of the property [who holds the deed] has the advantage.' But R. Yohanan ruled, 'Since the purchaser has come to remove property from the family, it is his burden to bring proof.' [Hence the purchaser, who holds the deed, is at a disadvantage.]"

[K]   He said to him, "I never said that."

[L]   Said R. Zira before R. Yosa, "Now even if R. Yohanan wants to deny [what is attributed to him]—did not R. Yannai [PM] state in the name of Rab(bi): 'The claim of the one who has a deed is subordinated'?" Said to him R. Yohanan, "And does not the Mishnah make this same point . . .' [above, III.A–B]?"

[M]   But [it is not a problem after all]. [Yohanan made his statement only to indicate that] sages accord with the view of Rab(bi). [But that is not his view of the decided law.]

[N]   R. Jeremiah in the name of Rab: "The law is in accord with the position of R. Meir."

[IV.A]   Samuel said, "The Mishnah has things reversed."

[B]   What is the meaning of this statement that the Mishnah has things reversed?

[C]   The older associates say, "Witnesses [are required by M. 9:6H–I]. [That is, the witnesses to the deed are interrogated as to the condition of the man who dictated the deed.]"

[D]   The younger associates say, "Witnesses are null, [and the testimony of those who have signed the deed is not solicited]."

[E]   Do they then dispute about the value of the testimony of the witnesses to the deed? [Why should there be such a dispute?]

[F]   Said R. Aha, "[The one who issued the deed rejects the witnesses:] 'Since to begin with I instructed you to write, '. . . who lies dying . . . ,' and you did not write it, you are liars,' [and the donor therefore declines to accept their testimony, one way or the other]."

The Talmud presents an extended and excellent discussion both of Mishnah and of Mishnah's implications. In many ways units I–III in the Talmud before us present a classic example of logical order for discussion. Unit I glosses Mishnah in important ways. Unit II then takes up the implications of Mishnah and compares them to a case which is parallel in principle but not in fact. The parallels are spelled out. Unit III takes up a detail of Mishnah and treats Mishnah's fact in a wholly fresh way, that is, the transfer of property through a deed. Mishnah now is relevant in fact but not parallel in principle. So the potentialities of exegesis—glossing, introduction of parallel principles in unrelated cases, discussion of the same facts in unrelated but intersecting areas of law—are amply worked out, as we move from Mishnah to quite distinct areas of discourse. Unit IV is a necessary clarification.

9:7   [In Leiden MS and *editio princeps* 9:9]

[A]   *He who verbally divides his property ["by word of mouth"]—*

[B]   *R. Eliezer says, "All the same are a healthy man and a man whose life is endangered—*

[C]   *"property for which there is security is acquired through money, a document, or usucaption.*

[D]   *"And that for which there is no security is acquired only through being drawn [into the possession of the one who acquires it]."*

[E]   *They said to him, "M^cSH B: The mother of the sons of Rokhel was sick and said, 'Give my veil to my daughter,' and it was worth twelve maneh. And she died, and sages carried out her statement."*

[F]   *He said to them, "As to the sons of Rokhel, may their mother bury them."*

[I.A]   Up to this point we have dealt with a case in which the movables and the real estate are in the same location.

[B]   But what if the movables are in one place and the real estate in some other? [How then is acquisition to be effected? Must the movables be located on the real property which is transferred?]

[C]   Said R. Bun, "Let us derive the answer to that question from the following:

[D]   **[Tosefta's version] Said R. Eliezer, "M^cSH B: There was a man from Meron in Jerusalem, who had a great many movables, and he wanted to give them [as a gift]. They said to him, 'You are not able to do so, [because you have no real property].' What did he do? He went and bought a single rock near Jerusalem, and said, 'The northern part of this [rock], and with it a hundred sheep and a hundred jugs of wine, are handed over to Mr. So-and-so. The southern part of this [rock], and with it a hundred sheep and a hundred jugs of wine, are handed over to Mr. Such-and-such. The eastern part of this rock, and with it, a hundred sheep and a hundred jugs of wine are handed over to Mr. So-and-so.'**

[E]   **"The case came before sages, and sages confirmed what he had said"** [T. B.B. 10:12]. [It follows from this story that the movables do not have to be located within the bounds of the real estate which is transferred.]

[F]   Said R. Hananiah before R. Mana, "Now was he not a dying man? [Eliezer cites the case, after all, for his argument that a dying man transfers ownership not verbally but only through the proper and established procedures. But the case then does not answer the question with which it has been cited to deal, because the rules pertinent to gifts in contemplation of death cannot be invoked in other contexts entirely, such as the one before us.]

[G]   "For under all circumstances a man transfers ownership only through a document, while here, he does so even verbally;

[H]   "[and, further,] in all other circumstances a person transfers ownership only when the real estate and the movables are located in a single place, while here, the real estate is in one location, while the movables are in another. [Consequently, as we said, this story does not prove the case.]"

[I]   He said to him, "And is it not a case involving R. Eliezer? Is there any difference between the two cases, for the laws governing the dying person, in the view of R. Eliezer, are the same as the laws governing a healthy person, in the view of the rabbis. [Consequently, the same law applies to the one and to the other, and, it follows, we may indeed derive the law governing the transfer of movables along with real estate in some other location.]"

[J]   [17b] He said to him, "[Yes, that is so]. The law governing a dying person in the view of R. Eliezer is the same as the law governing a healthy person in the view of rabbis, [and consequently the results of this inquiry are precisely as stated above]."

[K]   There we have learned: *R. Aqiba says, "Real estate of any size whatsoever is liable to the laws of peah and first fruits; a prozbol can be written on its security, and along with it movables can be acquired by money, writ, or usucaption"* [M. Pe. 3:6]. [Aqiba's statement indicates that movables need not be located on the property, since a piece of land of very small size is involved in his statement, and this then would be further evidence in behalf of the proposition under discussion.]

[L]   [Denying this conclusion,] said R. Mattenaiah, "But apply [Aqiba's statement] to the case of a space of ground sufficient for a single stalk of corn, under which a pearl is buried, [and it would not then follow that Aqiba in general maintains that the movables need not be located on the real property which is transferred; he may as well address the case described here, and no further conclusions are to be drawn]."

[II.A]   Said R. Yosé b. R. Bun, "[With regard to M. 9:7E–F,] Hila wanted to curse them, because they sow saffron in a vineyard."

Eliezer's position is that a verbal will is null, even if made by a dying man. Therefore there must be a proper act of acquisition of all property, C–D since the verbal will does not have the effect of imparting possession to the donees. Obviously, Eliezer can concur with M. 9:6, which speaks of only a written document. His opposition will maintain that a verbal will of a dying man is valid. The precedent, E, differs solely in terms of Eliezer's opinion. A verbal will of a dying person is valid. The discussion of unit **I** is not focused upon Mishnah at all. Tosefta's story, however, appears in conjunction with the present chapter of Mishnah, even though its issue is its own. It is only at **I**.I that we see why the case should be deemed pertinent to this pericope of Mishnah in particular. Unit **II** supplies a reason for Eliezer's curse.

9:8   [In Leiden MS and *editio princeps* 9:10–11]

[A]   *And sages say, "[If he gave verbal instructions] on the Sabbath, his statement is confirmed,*

[B]   *"because he is not able to write down [his will].*

[C]   *"But not [if it took place] on a weekday."*

[D]   *R. Joshua says, "[If] they have stated this rule for the Sabbath, all the more so should it apply on a weekday."*

[E]   *Similarly:*

[F]   *Others may effect possession for a minor, but they do not effect possession for an adult.*

[G]   *R. Joshua says, "If they have said so of a minor, all the more so does the rule apply to an adult."*

[I.A]   There are Tannaim who teach matters the opposite [namely, if the verbal will is made on an ordinary weekday, it is valid, but not on the Sabbath].

[B]   [Supporting the present reading,] R. Joshua b. Levi said, "Thus does the Mishnah read: *If they have stated this rule for the Sabbath, all the more so should it apply on a weekday* [and consequently, the reading before us is the only possible one]."

[C]   There are Tannaim who teach the opposite [at F].

[D]   [Supporting the present reading,] R. Joshua b. Levi said, "Thus
       does the Mishnah read: *If they have said so of a minor, all the
       more so does the rule apply to an adult*," [with the same conse-
       quence as at B].

Sages make a distinction between weekday and Sabbath. They
concur with Eliezer, M. 9:7, that a verbal will made on a weekday is null. But if it is made on the Sabbath, it is valid, for the
reason made explicit at B. Joshua maintains that a verbal will is
valid, whenever it is made. Whether he also maintains that the
healthy man as much as the sick man can impart acquisition
through a verbal donation is not specified. The argument of D
suggests, however, that that is the case. The point of Joshua's
two arguments is simple. In the case of the verbal instructions,
he argues that if the verbal will made on the Sabbath is valid, so
that no written deed or act of possession is required, when these
things in any event may not be carried out at all, it should surely
be the case that a verbal will or donation done on a weekday
should be valid, when these things may be done. In the case of
allowing possession to be done in behalf of a minor and also of
an adult, Joshua constructs a similar argument. If an act of possession may be done in behalf of a minor, who himself cannot
effect such an action, all the more so it should be permitted in
behalf of an adult, who is subject to a less severe status, in that
he may indeed effect acquisition or appoint an agent to do so in
his behalf. The Talmud confirms the readings before us, by
showing that the reasoning of Joshua is possible only on the
strength of Mishnah's reading as we now have it.

9:9   [In Leiden MS and *editio princeps* 9:12–14]

[A]   *[If] the house fell on him and on his father,*

[B]   *or on him and on those whom he inherits,*

[C]   *and he was liable for the settlement of his wife's marriage con-
       tract and for payment of a debt—*

[D]   *the heirs of the father claim, "The son died first, and then the
       father died"—*

[E]   *the creditors claim, "The father died first, and then the son"—*

[F]   *the House of Shammai say, "Let them share [the son's estate]."*

[G]   *And the House of Hillel say, "The property remains in its former status [in the hands of those who inherit the father]."*

[H]   *[If] the house fell on him and on his wife,*

[I]   *the heirs of the husband say, "The wife died first, and afterward the husband died"—*

[J]   *the heirs of the wife say, "The husband died first, and afterward the wife died"—*

[K]   *the House of Shammai say, "Let them divide."*

[L]   *And the House of Hillel say, "The property remains in its former status.*

[M]   *"The money for the marriage settlement remains in the hands of the heirs of the husband.*

[N]   *"But the property which goes into the marriage with her and goes out of the marriage with her [at the value at which it was assessed to begin with] is assigned to the possession of the heirs of the father [of the wife]."*

[O]   *[If] the house fell on him and on his mother—*

[P]   *these and those parties agree that they divide it.*

[Q]   *Said R. Aqiba, "I concur in this case that the property remains in its former status."*

[R]   *Ben Azzai said to him, "Concerning the points of difference we are distressed.*

[S]   *"Will you now come to bring disagreement on the points on which they are in agreement?"*

[I.A]   Said R. Samuel b. R. Isaac, "That is to say that [by using "you," rather than, "our rabbi,"] Ben Azzai [speaks] as both a colleague and disciple to R. Aqiba."

Effectively there is no Talmud to M. 9:9.

10:1

[A]   *An unfolded document [has] the signatures within [at the bot-tom of a single page of writing].*

[B]   *And one which is folded has the signatures behind [each fold].*

[C]   *An unfolded document, on which its witnesses signed at the back,*

[D]   *or a folded document, on which its witnesses signed on the in-side—*

[E]   *either of them is invalid.*

[F]   *R. Hananiah b. Gamaliel says, "One which is folded, on the inside of which its witnesses signed their names, is valid,*

[G]   *"because one can unfold it."*

[H]   *Rabban Simeon b. Gamaliel says, "Everything is in accord with local custom."*

[II.A]   [17c] And how do we know that there is a document which is folded [and another which is unfolded]?

[B]   Said R. Imi, " 'Then I took the sealed deed of purchase, con-taining the terms and conditions, and the open copy . . .' (Jer. 32:11).

[C]   " 'The sealed deed of purchase'—this is the folded document.

[D]   " '. . . and the open copy . . . ,'—this is the unfolded one which is within the folded one.

[E]   " '. . . the terms and conditions . . .'—[what is the difference] between the one [unfolded] and the other [folded]?

[F]   "But: This one bears two [witnesses], and the other, three [M. 10:2].

[G]   "In this one the witnesses sign on the inside, and in the other, on the outside."

[H]   [Answering A,] And the rabbis of Caesarea say, " 'Then I took the sealed deed of purchase, containing the terms and conditions, and the open copy . . .'

[I]   " 'The deed of purchase'—this is the unfolded one.

[J]   " 'The sealed one'—this is the folded one.

[K]   " 'And the open copy'—this is the unfolded one which is within the folded one.

[L]   " 'The terms and conditions . . .'—[what is the difference] between the one and the other?

[M]   "But: This one bears two [witnesses], and the other, three.

[N]   "In this one the witnesses sign on the inside, and in the other, on the outside."

[II.A]   R. Idi in the name of R. Jeremiah: "The law covering the folded document is as follows:

[B]   "One writes the name of the lender, the name of the borrower, the name of the witnesses, and the date.

[C]   "He then folds it and goes and writes the same thing below."

[III.A]   [Translating the version of Y. Git. 8:10:] R. Ba in the name of R. Judah: "In an unfolded document its witnesses [sign] along its breadth. In a folded document, its witnesses sign along its length."

[B]   Said R. Idi, "The witnesses sign between one fold and another, and that is on condition that it is above [on the upper of the two sides of the fold]."

[C]   And should we not take into consideration the possibility of counterfeit [in the case of a folded document, if the witnesses sign at the top and between the folds but not at the bottom]?

[D]   Said R. Huna in reply, "The witnesses never sign the document at the bottom until they read what is written in it on the top:

[E]   "'I, So-and-so, son of Such-and-such, accept upon me responsibility for all which is written in this document above.'"

[IV.A]   R. Ba in the name of R. Jeremiah: "The names of the witnesses must be two lines below the body of the text of the document."

[B]   R. Idi in the name of R. Jeremiah: "In a folded document, the names of the witnesses are written lengthwise.

[C]   "In an unfolded document the names of the witnesses are written breadthwise, one inside and one outside."

[D]   [Following PM, we delete: "How does one carry it out?"]

[E]   Said R. Mana, "How do the witnesses sign in the case of a writ of divorce which is folded?"

[F]   Said R. Huna, "Between each fold, and that is on condition that it be at the top [of the fold]."

[G]   Said R. Idi, "And that is on condition that between the name of the witnesses and the writ itself should not be a space of two lines."

[H]   Simeon bar Vava in the name of R. Yohanan: "If one has set aside those two lines for some other matter, [the document is null] even if it is any small item at all. [That is, no other item may intervene between the body of the text and the signatures of the witnesses.]"

[I]   Said R. Samuel b. R. Isaac, "The Mishnah itself has said so:

[J]   *"If the signature of one is written in Hebrew and one in Greek, one in Hebrew and one in Greek, running from under this [writ] to that one, both of them are invalid* [M. Git. 9:6E–F],

[K]   "for do they not deal with some other matter [than the one with which the document is meant to serve]? [This proves the point of H.]"

[L]   [Tosefta's version] **[If the witnesses signed two or three lines below the body of the text, it is invalid. (If they signed) closer than this (to the body of the text), it is valid.] And how far [may their names appear] below the text [of the document] for the document to be valid?**

[M]   **"Sufficient so that [their names] may be read right along with the text," the words of Rabbi.**

[N]   **R. Simeon b. Eleazar says, "The distance of one line."**

[O]   **R. Dosetai b. R. Yannai says, "The distance of the signatures of two witnesses"** [T. B.B. 11:10].

[P]   R. Jeremiah said in the name of Rab, "They estimate [the appropriate distance between two lines by providing a space so that, on the adjacent lines, the letters] LK LK [may be written one on top of the other without actually touching]."

[Q]   By what script do they make the stated estimate?

[R]   R. Yosa in the name of R. Shobetai: "The size of the signatures of the witnesses. [That is, the letters LK LK are written according to the way in which the witnesses write those letters.]"

[S]   Hezekiah said, "But that is on condition that the result is a lenient decision.

[T]   "So if the signature of the witnesses is small, and the writing is large [that is, the writing of the body of the document], they follow the size of the large script. If the signature of the witnesses is large and the writing is small, they follow the small script. [A counterfeiter will want to reproduce the style of the witnesses (PM).]"

[U]   Said R. Isaac, "If the name is one such as Yosé b. Yannai [lacking the letters LK], they make the estimate so that the words MLK [King] and BN MLK (Prince) [may be written on top of one another without the K's touching one another]."

[V]   Said R. Idi in the name of R. Jeremiah, "One has to keep a space between the body of a document and an erasure [on the same parchment, that is, a palimpsest] a distance of two lines [so that the scribe writes and the witnesses sign on the space on which there is no prior writing, to avoid the possibility of erasing yet another time and writing whatever one likes]."

[W]   Said R. Isaac, "That rule applies [not only to a folded document, in which, to begin with, the witnesses sign on the outside, but even to] an unfolded one."

[V.A]   Rab said, "If there is an erasure or an interlinear insertion in a document—this is [subject to] its confirmation. [That is, one has to write at the end of the document that such-and-such a word has been erased, or such-and-such a letter has been inserted.

This then serves to validate the document, even with the erasure or insertion.]"

[B]   Rab said, "This is subject to confirmation [as explained above]."

[C]   R. Abbahu in the name of R. Isaac b. Haqola: "Whatever you can assign to an erasure should be assigned to the erasure. [The meaning of this statement is explained presently.]"

[D]   What is the meaning of this statement, "Whatever you can assigned to the erasure"?

[E]   R. Yosé the fuller, son-in-law of R. Yosah, in the name of R. Yosah: "A codicil is written above [which states, in a deed of betrothal, 'I betroth you with the condition that I may marry you on a certain day, and if that day arrives and I do not marry you, I shall have no claim on you,'] and a codicil is erased below.

[F]   "I maintain [in interpreting this document] that they decided to complete the transaction as a final act of betrothal [of the woman]. [There then was no stipulation or condition attached to the writ. They then erased it.] So as not to disturb the document, they simply erased the codicil. [This is an example of assigning to an erasure whatever one can. In this case the stipulation was ultimately rejected and so erased, with the result that the codicil described at E is deemed to have been rejected and nullified by the erasure. The document then attests to a formal and final act of betrothal.]"

[G]   And rabbis take into consideration not disturbing the document [and so gave instructions not to make interlinear insertions in the documents if these can be avoided].

[H]   A bill of indebtedness went from R. Huna [who made no decision on it] to R. Shimi, on which the word *ogdoé* [of *ogdoeconta*, eighty] was erased, and *conta* was clear.

[I]   Said R. Shimi to R. Huna, "Go and see what is the lowest numeral in Greek that *conta* is combined with."

[J]   He said, "It is *triaconta* [thirty]."

[K]   When the party had left, he said, "That man intended to make thirty [by the erasure] and lost twenty [the original was fifty, *penteconta*]." [Following Jastrow, p. 21a.]

[**VI**.A] [With reference to M. 10:1C–F: *Hananiah b. Gamaliel says, "One which is folded, on the inside of which its witnesses signed their names, is valid, because one can unfold it,"*] Rabbi replied with the intention of supporting the position of R. Hananiah b. Gamaliel, "The body of a document indicates its character, that is, whether the document is unfolded or is not folded."

[B] What is the meaning of "the body of the document"?

[C] Said R. Ba, "It is that which Huna said: 'The witnesses never sign the document at the bottom until they read what is written in it on the top: I, So-and-so, son of Such-and-such, accept upon me responsibility for all which is written in this document above.' [This is what is written in the body of a folded document, which then cannot be confused with an unfolded one.]"

[D] Now has it not been taught: The formula of deeds is thus [that is, precisely the language Huna says]. [That formula will appear in an unfolded, as much as in a folded, writ. Consequently, the body of the document will not indicate the character thereof, folded or unfolded.]

[E] Said R. Mani, "[The cited tradition is:] 'The formula of *folded* deeds [only] is thus,' [and the presence of that formula proves precisely what Rabbi says it proves, since it can be only in a folded document]."

[F] Said R. Abin, "And even if you say that the unfolded and the folded documents are alike [in containing the cited language], in an unfolded document, the absence of that language disqualifies a document, but in a folded one, the absence of that language does not constitute a disqualification. [So the proof does not hold.]"

[G] R. Judah says, "It is as if one has added to the required law [of making up such a document]. [The body of the document will not prove that it is an unfolded or a folded document. Even if we find the language which would signify that it is a folded document, one may say that it was originally an unfolded document, but the writer added language beyond what the law requires. It would be comparable to adding to the number of witnesses.] [That is to say,] an unfolded document has two witnesses, and a folded one has three, but they have [taken an unfolded document and had] three witnesses [sign it, even though that is not required by the law].

[H]   "[Or it would be tantamount to taking] a document which was
      unfolded on the inside and folded at the outside [that is, con-
      formed to the rules governing the unfolded deed on the inside,
      and to the rules governing the folded deed at the outside], and
      they made the witnesses sign on both the inside and the outside.
      [Consequently, these are mere improvements on the document
      and will not signify the original character thereof. So Hananiah
      b. Gamaliel's position is not to be supported as Rabbi has at-
      tempted to do.]"

There are two distinct kinds of legal documents, one which is
written on one side of the document only, an unfolded document, used for deeds or notes, and a special form of deed, the
folded one. This is written on alternate lines, separated by blank
ones. Each line was folded over a blank one and the successive
pairs were stitched together. We go over the matter of appropriate signatures. The unfolded deed bears its signatures at the bottom of the page; a folded one has witnesses sign behind each
fold. A variation in this requirement invalidates the document.
An insufficient number of witnesses invalidates the document.
The glosses of M. 10:1F–G and H are clear as stated. Hananiah
has the notion that one can always turn a folded document into a
flat one by unstitching it. The Talmud's discussion follows a program of asking the most fundamental and factual questions in
clarification of Mishnah. The first is the source of the stated distinction between documents, unit **I**. Unit **II** proceeds to provide
the formula for the folded deed. Unit **III**, presented as it is at Y.
Git. 8:10, discusses the location of the signatures of the witnesses in the two types of documents and takes up the question
of the possibility of forgery or counterfeit of their names. Unit
IV continues with this question of the location of the signatures
of the witnesses, with attention to the verification of the number
of lines in the document. The next question, unit **V**, is on the
presence of erasures, a matter which we shall confront in Mishnah below. Of special interest here is the erasure of a codicil
changing the stipulations of a document of betrothal, V.E–G.
A case on how we interpret erasures, V.H–K, further clarifies
what is at issue; my translation is taken from Jastrow, as indicated. Unit **VI**, finally, explores the position attempted by Hananiah b. Gamaliel and rejects it as impossible in accord with the
decided law.

10:2

[A]   *An unfolded document—its witnesses are two.*

[B]   *And a folded one—its witnesses are three.*

[C]   *An unfolded one in which there is a single witness,*

[D]   *and a folded one in which there are two witnesses—*

[E]   *both of them are invalid.*

[F]   *[If] there was written in a bond of indebtedness, "A hundred zuz, which are twenty selas," [the creditor] has a claim on only twenty selas [even though a hundred zuz are twenty-five selas].*

[G]   *[If it is written,] "A hundred zuz which are thirty selas," he has a claim only on a maneh [a hundred zuz], [since a hundred zuz are twenty-five selas].*

[H]   *"Silver zuzim which are . . . ," and the rest was blotted out—*

[I]   *there is a claim of no less than two.*

[J]   *"Silver selas which are . . . ," and the rest was blotted out— there is a claim of no less than two.*

[K]   *"Darics which are . . . ," and the rest was blotted out—there is a claim for no less than two.*

[I.A]   It was taught, [If in a document is written,] ". . . zuzim, which are . . . ," and the rest is blotted out—

[B]   [the lender claims] five, and the other party says that they are only two [which he owes], [does this constitute concession of part of a claim, entailing an oath covering the rest of it?]

[C]   There they say, Ben Azzai and R. Aqiba—

[D]   one said, "He pays two, and takes an oath covering the rest."

[E]   And the other said, "Since, had he conceded nothing whatsoever, he would have received only two, the borrower takes an oath only covering the sum which he concedes. [Since the deed conforms to the statement of the borrower, there is no substantive concession whatsoever.]"

The Talmud raises an important amplificatory question.

10:3

[A]   *[If] written at the top is, "a maneh," and at the bottom "two hundred zuz,"*

[B]   *or at the top, "two hundred zuz," and at the bottom, "maneh"—*

[C]   *all follows what is written at the bottom.*

[D]   *If so, why do they write the upper figure at all?*

[E]   *So that if the lower figure is blotted out, one may learn [may infer] from the upper figure [the sum covered by the bond].*

[I.A] **It was taught: Under all circumstances what is written below may learn [be inferred] from what is written above [M. 10:2E];**

[B]   **in the case of a folded writ, from a single sign, not from two signs,**

[C]   **whether Hanan or Hanani, whether Anan or Anani,**

[D]   **on the strength of a single mark they confirm it,**

[E]   **and on the strength of two marks they do not confirm it [T. B.B. 11:4].**

[F]   R. Isaac asked, "[If] above it is written, Hanan, and below, Nani [a diminutive], what is the law?

[G]   "Do we infer what belongs below from what is written above, [and hence assign the debt to] Hanan, or in this case do we learn what belongs above from what is written below, [and hence assign the debt to] Nani?" [This question is not answered.]

The Talmud performs its simplest operation: a citation of a relevant passage of Tosefta, a proposed inquiry which is not carried forward.

10:4

[A]   *They write out a writ of divorce for a man, even though his wife is not with him.*

[B]   *And a quittance for the wife, even though her husband is not with her,*

[C]   *on condition that [the scribe] knows them.*

[D]   *And the husband pays the fee.*

[E]   *They write a writ of indebtedness for the borrower, even though the lender is not with him,*

[F]   *but they do not write a writ for the lender, unless the borrower is with him.*

[G]   *The borrower pays the scribe's fee.*

[H]   *They write a writ of sale for the seller, even though the buyer is not with him.*

[I]   *But they do not write a writ of sale for the purchaser, unless the seller is with him.*

[J]   *And the purchaser pays the scribe's fee.*

[K]   *They write the documents of betrothal and marriage only with the knowledge and consent of both parties.*

[L]   *And the husband pays the scribe's fee.*

[M]   *They write documents of tenancy and sharecropping only with the knowledge and consent of both parties.*

[N]   *And the tenant pays the scribe's fee.*

[O]   *They write documents of arbitration or any document drawn up before a court only with the knowledge and consent of both litigants.*

[P]   *And both litigants pay the scribe's fee.*

[Q]   *Rabban Simeon b. Gamaliel says, "They write two for the two parties, one copy for each."*

[I.A]   Said R. Ba, "[With reference to M. 10:4C,] [the scribe] has to know both of them [when writing the writ of divorce for the wife, he must know her as well as the husband; when writing the quittance for the husband, he must know him as well as the wife]."

[B]   Said R. La, "He must know the husband when he is writing the writ of divorce for him [to give to the wife], and the wife when he is writing her quittance [to be given to the husband, but in the former case he need not know the wife, and in the latter, the husband]."

[C] The Mishnah stands at variance with the position of R. Ba: "[At first he used to change his name and her name, the name of his town and the name of her town] [that is, given an adopted name]. And Rabban Gamaliel the Elder ordained that one should write, "Mr. So-and-so and whatever alias he may have," "Mrs. So-and-so and whatever alias she may have," for the good order of the world [M. Git. 4:2]. [If the scribe knows both of them, then why should he change their names? He would not agree to do so if he knew them. La can deal with this passage, since, so far as he is concerned, the scribe need not know the woman. So there was need to make sure the woman's name was not changed, and, along the way, the ordinance covered the husband as well.]

[D] And even in accord with the view of R. La, the cited pericope of Mishnah poses no problems: At first he used to change his name and her name, the name of his town and the name of her town [and La can explain this statement, as noted above].

The Talmud deals with only one detail of Mishnah. A better version of this discussion is at Y. Git. 4:2.

10:5   [In Leiden MS and *editio princeps* 10:5-7]

[A] *He who paid part of a debt which he owed and who deposited the bond with a third party,*

[B] *to whom he said, "If I have not given you [what I still owe the lender] between now and such-and-such a date, give [the creditor] his bond of indebtedness,"*

[C] *[if] the time came, and he has not paid,*

[D] *R. Yosé says, "He should hand it over."*

[E] *And R. Judah says, "He should not hand it over."*

[F] *He whose writ of indebtedness was blotted out—*

[G]   witnesses give testimony about it,

[H]   and he comes to a court, and they draw up this confirmation:

[I]   *"Mr. So-and-so, son of So-and-so—his bond of indebtedness was blotted out on such-and-such a day, and Mr. So-and-so and Mr. Such-and-such are his witnesses."*

[I.A]   It was taught: As to a promise made with the condition of a forfeit in case of a failure to fulfill it—

[B]   R. Abbahu orders collection [on such a surety].

[C]   R. Aha orders collection likewise.

[D]   R. Ami orders collection likewise.

[E]   R. Jonah and R. Yosé do not order collection [of such a surety].

[F]   Said R. Mana, "Even though R. Yosé [E] declares sureties of this sort not to be collectible, he concedes that they are collectible in the case of those who indenture their sons to a trade, [because the livelihood of men requires such a measure]" [Jastrow, p. 1074a].

[II.A]   Said R. Uqba, "The stated rule [M. 10:5F] applies also to documents covering marriage settlements."

[B]   Members of the House of Levi state: "He who says, 'My deed has been lost [not merely blotted out]'—a court draws up a confirmation of the original document."

[C]   It was taught: Rabban Simeon b. Gamaliel says, "Even in the case of writs of arbitration [in which each party agrees to have the case arbitrated by judges on whom they will concur], a court provides a confirmation of the original document."

Unit **I** goes over the legal instrumentality parallel to the one of our pericope of Mishnah, and indicates positions parallel to those of Yosé and Judah. Those who maintain such a surety is collectible will concur with Yosé, and those who maintain the contrary, with Judah. Unit **II** extends the court procedure for confirming erased documents to those that are lost, and also to documents other than the writ of indebtedness to which Mishnah makes reference.

10:6   [In Leiden MS and *editio princeps* 10:8–12]

[A]   *He who had paid off part of his debt—*

[B]   *R. Judah says, "He should exchange [the bond for another one, in which what is now owing is specified]."*

[C]   *R. Yosé says, "[The creditor] should write him a receipt [for what has been paid]."*

[D]   *Said R. Judah, "It turns out that this one [the debtor] has to guard his receipt from rats."*

[E]   *Said to him R. Yosé, "That's good for him, so long as the right of the other party [the creditor] has not been damaged."*

[I.A]   [As to Judah's statement, that he should exchange the bond for another one, M. 10:6B,] Rab said, "The court provides a confirmation for him."

[B]   R. Hiyya taught, "It is not the court [alone] which provides a confirmation for him, [but even the witnesses to the original document may do so]."

[C]   Said R. Jeremiah, "If Rab had heard this teaching [of Hiyya], he would not have made the statement that he did [requiring that the court alone supply the confirmation]."

[II.A]   [The confirmation is as follows:] For example, they say the following, "I, Mr. So-and-so, son of Such-and-such, borrow from you, Mr. So-and-so; and Mr. Such-and-such serves as surety for this loan."

[B]   Rab said, "He must mention the date of the [17d] first document in the second one."

[C]   And Samuel said, "He does not have to mention the date of the first document in the second."

[D]   R. Hiyya taught, "One does not have to mention the date of the first document in the second."

[E]   R. Yohanan raised the question of whether one has to mention the date of the first document in the second, in the light of the following statement of R. Yosé: *"That's good for him, so long as the right of the other party has not been damaged."* [This would protect the right of the lender to collect his debt by seizing property sold by the borrower to others between the time of the first

and the second deed, since the earlier date of the actual loan still
is easily proved. Now if one indeed has to include the date of the
first deed in the second, as Rab maintains, then why should Yosé
have made the cited statement?]"

Judah favors the debtor, Yosé the creditor, as at M. 10:5D and
E explain the positions of each. What is troubling Yosé is this. If
there is a new writ, bearing a later date than the old, then, if the
debtor defaults, the creditor will not be able to seize property
sold by the debtor from the day on which the first writ was written to the day on which the second writ (the new one) was written. By postdating the loan, the writ of indebtedness thus limits
the possibilities for the collection from indentured and then
alienated property of what is defaulted. Unit **I** clarifies Judah's
opinion, M. 10:6B, explaining who issues the proposed document. Unit **II** is relevant to Mishnah only at **II.E.**

10:7   [In Leiden MS and *editio princeps* 10:11–13]

[A]   *Two brothers—*

[B]   *one poor, one rich—*

[C]   *their father left them a bathhouse and an olive-press—*

[D]   *[if] the father had built them to rent them out—*

[E]   *the rent is held in common.*

[F]   *[If] he made them for his own use,*

[G]   *lo, the rich one says to the poor one, "You buy the slaves, and
let them wash in the bathhouse."*

[H]   *"You buy olives, and come and prepare them in the olive-press."*

[I]   *Two who were in the same town—*

[J]   *the name of one was Joseph b. Simeon, and the name of the
other was Joseph b. Simeon—*

[K]   *they cannot produce a writ of indebtedness against one another,*

[L]   *nor can a third party produce a writ of indebtedness against
either one of them.*

[M]   *[If] among the documents of one of them is found a writ of Joseph b. Simeon which has been paid off, the writs of both of them are deemed to have been paid off.*

[N]   *What should they do?*

[O]   *Let them write down the names of the third generation.*

[P]   *And if all three [generations'] names are alike, let them write a description.*

[Q]   *And if the descriptions are alike, let them write, "Priest."*

[R]   *He who says to his son, "There is a bond of indebtedness among my documents which has been paid, and I do not know which one of them it is"—all of his bonds are deemed to have been paid off.*

[S]   *[If] two were found applying to a single [debtor],*

[T]   *the larger one is deemed to have been paid, and the smaller one is not deemed to have been paid.*

[I.A]   It was taught: The concern for paying off a deed covering a large sum of money is not the same as that for paying off a deed covering a small sum of money. [The former is likely to be paid off first.]

The Talmud explains M. 10:7T.

10:8   [In Leiden MS and *editio princeps* 10:14]

[A]   *He who lends money to his fellow on the strength of a guarantor may not collect from the guarantor.*

[B]   *But if he had said, "[Lo, I lend to you] on condition that I may collect from whichever party I wish," he may then collect from the guarantor.*

[C]   *Rabban Simeon b. Gamaliel says, "If the debtor has property, one way or the other, he should not collect from the guarantor."*

[I.A]   R. Abbahu in the name of R. Yohanan, "[As to the dispute of M. 10:8B, C,] When the borrower has property, [the lender collects from him]. But if the borrower has no property, he may collect from the guarantor.

[B] *"And if he had said, 'Lo, I lend to you on condition that I may collect from whichever party I wish,' he may then collect from the guarantor,*

[C] "even if the borrower has property."

[II.A] There they say, "In every case the law is in accord with the position of Rabban Simeon b. Gamaliel, except for the matter of the pledge [the present rule]; the case of Sidon [M. Git. 7:5]; and the matter of bringing proof after a trial is concluded [M. San. 3:8]."

[B] They say, "That fact is so for only what he says in the Mishnah of ours, [but not in an external tradition (*baraita*)]."

[C] R. Ami bar Qorha in the name of Rab: "And why have they said that in every case the law is in accord with the position of Rabban Simeon b. Gamaliel? For he would state decided law as presented by his court [and not only his private opinion]."

Unit **I** clarifies what is at issue in the language of Mishnah's dispute, and unit **II** supplements M. 10:8.

10:9   [In Leiden MS and *editio princeps* 10:15]

[A] *And so did Rabban Simeon b. Gamaliel say, "Also: he who was guarantor for a woman as to her marriage settlement, and her husband divorced her—*

[B] *"[in the case of a divorce] let the husband vow not to derive benefit from her,*

[C] *"lest they make a conspiracy to defraud this one of his property,*

[D] *"and [the husband] then remarry his wife."*

[I.A] The father-in-law of the daughter of R. Haggai was guarantor for the marriage contract for the daughter of R. Haggai. Now she treated his property wastefully, [so her husband wanted to divorce her]. The case came before R. Aha. He said, "The husband has to vow not to derive benefit from her [= M. 10:9B]."

[B]   Said R. Yosé, "He does not have to vow not to derive benefit from her." [Yosé does not suspect the husband and wife of conspiracy against the guarantor of the marriage settlement.]

[C]   Associates say before R. Yosé, "And what will happen if the husband again goes and marries her? Will not her debtors come and seize the property [of the guarantor of the marriage settlement, in settlement of her debts owing to them]?"

[D]   He replied, "[What difference does it make?] If he does not remarry her, in any case they may transfer the property to movables [which are not subject to collection by the creditors], or they will treat the property as an 'iron flock' [which the woman cannot squander away]. Accordingly, the creditors will not find anything to seize."

[E]   The case nonetheless was settled in accord with the view of R. Aha.

The Talmud provides an admirable illustration to Mishnah's rule about the possibilities of fraud.

10:10   [In Leiden MS and *editio princeps* 10:16–17]

[A]   *He who lends money to his fellow on the security of a bond of indebtedness collects what is owing to him from mortgaged property.*

[B]   *[But if he had lent to him on the security only of] witnesses, he collects only from unindentured property.*

[C]   *[If] he produced against him [the debtor's] note of hand [as evidence] that he owes him [money],*

[D]   *he collects from unindentured property.*

[E]   *He who signs as guarantor below the [signature of] bonds of indebtedness—[the creditor] collects [only] from unindentured property.*

[F]   *A case came before R. Ishmael, and he ruled, "He may collect from unindentured property."*

[G]   *Said to him Ben Nannos, "He collects neither from mortgaged property nor from unindentured property."*

[H]   *He said to him, "Why?"*

[I]   *He said to him, "He who seizes someone by the throat [who owes him money] in the market, and his fellow came upon him and said to him, 'Let him go and I'll pay you'—[the latter] is exempt [from having to guarantee the loan],*

[J]   *"since it was not in reliance upon him that he had lent [the debtor] the money [in the first place]."*

[K]   *"But who is the guarantor who is liable [to pay if the debtor does not do so]?*

[L]   *"[One who says,] 'Lend him money, and I'll pay you back'—*

[M]   *"he is liable.*

[N]   *"For it was in reliance upon him that he had lent [the debtor] the money [in the first place]."*

[O]   *Said R. Ishmael, "He who wants to get smart had best get busy with commercial law.*

[P]   *"For you have no specialty in the Torah greater than those laws.*

[Q]   *"For they are like an ever-bubbling spring.*

[R]   *"He who wants to get busy with commercial law had best serve [as disciple of] Simeon b. Nannos."*

[I.A]   [With reference to M. Sheb. 10:5: *A predated prozbul is valid, but a postdated one is invalid. A predated bond is not valid, but a postdated bond is valid.* At Y. Sheb. 10:3, R. Yohanan said, "It is totally invalid (and not collectible). R. Simeon b. Laqish said, 'It is treated as valid only from the point at which it was actually written" but it is in fact collectible.] [Concurring with the position of Simeon b. Laqish,] R. Huna said, "The predating is invalid, but the deed is valid [and may be collected]."

[B]   Now have we not learned in the Mishnah: *A predated prozbul is valid, but a postdated one is invalid* [so far as the later date, but it is valid so far as protecting the right of the creditor to collect his debts contracted prior to the correct date of the document]? [This then supports Huna's view.]

[C]   That which you have assigned to R. Huna is in accord with R. Eleazar.

And so said R. Simeon b. Yaqim, "That which is assigned to R. Huna is in accord with R. Eleazar who said, 'Even though there are no witnesses [on the writ of divorce], but they handed it over to her in the presence of witnesses, the writ of divorce is valid, and the wife may collect her marriage settlement from mortgaged property. For witnesses sign on the writ of divorce only for the good order of the world.'"

[D]   Now how [is this matter of the predated deed to be dealt with]?

[E]   If we deal with a case in which the witnesses denied their testimony, the one who denied his testimony is as if he were not present, and does the writ remain valid in any event?

[F]   "But we deal with a witness who did not deny their testimony. [Then that testimony remains valid.]"

[G]   "But lo, R. Simeon b. Laqish said, 'They have treated the witnesses who have signed on a deed as those whose testimony has been carefully tested in court.'" [So if the deed is valid, it is for Eleazar's reason at C.]

[H]   [As to R. Simeon b. Laqish's position, who concurs with R. Huna that they count only from the actually writing of the writ, and that the writ may be used to collect a deed from its correct date,] what is then the rule?

[I]   We deal with a case involving those who say the following: "I, Mr. So-and-so, son of Mr. Such-and-such, have borrowed from Mr. So-and-so, and Mr. Such-and-such is guarantor." [There is no need of testimony in this case.]

[J]   Rab said, "He has to make mention of the date of the first writ on the second."

[K]   And Samuel said, "He does not have to make mention of the date of the first writ deed on the second."

[L]   Rab and Samuel—

[M]   Rab is in accord with R. Yohanan, and Samuel is in accord with R. Simeon b. Laqish.

[II.A]   R. Yosa in the name of R. Yohanan said, "Even though R. Ishmael has praised Ben Nannos for his exposition, the law is not in accord with Ben Nannos."

[B]   Simeon bar Vava in the name of R. Yohanan: "Even in the case of one who is being strangled in the market place, the law is in accord with R. Ishmael."

[C]   Said R. Yosé, "And you derive from that rule the following: Another one came along and said, 'Leave him alone, and I'll give you what he owes.' Does the creditor collect from the latter, and from the other does he not collect?"

Unit **I** serves Y. Sheb. 10:3 and is dealt with there. Only unit **II** serves the present pericope of Mishnah, and its point is clear as stated. Yosé's question is not answered.

Abbreviations, Bibliography, and Glossary

Ah: Ahilot = ohalot.

Am haares: An Israelite who is not trusted properly to tithe his produce or to observe the rules of Levitical cleanness. The opposite of a *haber*.

Amah: A cubit (pl.: *amot*).

Appointed Times: Jacob Neusner. *A History of the Mishnaic Law of Appointed Times*. 5 vols. Leiden: E. J. Brill, 1980–81.

Ar.: Arakhin.

Asherah: A tree worshiped in idolatry.

A.Z.: Abodah Zarah.

b.: *Babli*, Babylonian Talmud; *ben*, "son of."

B.B.: Baba Batra.

Bek: Bekhorot.

Ber.: Berakhot.

Bes.: Besah.

Bet hammidrash: Schoolhouse (lit., house of study).

Bet haperas: A field declared unclean on account of crushed bones spread through it from a plowed-up grave.

Bet kor: 75,000 square cubits, the area of land in which a *kor* of seed is planted.

Bet roba: The area of land in which one quarter *qab* of seed is planted, approximately 104 square cubits.

Bet seah: The area of land in which a *seah* of seed is planted, 2,500 square cubits.

Bik.: Bikkurim.

B.M.: Baba Mesia.

Bokser: Baruch M. Bokser. "An Annotated Bibliographical Guide to the Study of the Palestinian Talmud." In Wolfgang Haase, ed., *Principat* (*ANRW* II. 19.2). Berlin and New York, 1979. Pp. 139–256.

B.Q.: Baba Qamma.

Chron.: Chronicles.

Comm.: Commentary.

Damages: Jacob Neusner. *A History of the Mishnaic Law of Damages*. 5 vols. Leiden: E. J. Brill, 1983–85.

Daric: a coin.

Dem.: Demai.

Demai: Produce about which there is doubt whether or not the required heave offering and tithes were removed.

Denar: A coin worth one half *shekel*.

Deut.: Deuteronomy.

Diverse kinds: Heterogeneous plants or animals. These may not be joined together through being planted in the same field, harnessed together, or cross-bred (Lev. 19:19, Deut. 22:9–11).

Dupondium: A coin worth one-twelfth of a *shekel*.

Ed.: Eduyyot.

Eighteen Benedictions: The central prayer of the liturgy, recited three times daily, four times on Sabbaths and festivals, and five times on the Day of Atonement.

Erub: A deposit of food which is used (1) to amalgamate several distinct domains or (2) to establish a temporary abode. As a result, on the sabbath, individuals freely may cross the boundaries of the distinct domains or move beyond the usual range of 2,000 cubits permitted for movement on the holy day.

Erub.: Erubin.

Etrog: A citron carried on the Festival of Boothes as the "fruit of goodly trees," mentioned at Lev. 23:40.

Exod.: Exodus.

Ezek.: Ezekiel.

Francus: Israel Francus. *Talmud Yerushalmi. Massekhet Besah. Im perush . . . Eleazar Azkari.* New York: Feldheim, 1967.

Gen.: Genesis.

Ginzberg: Louis Ginzberg. *Yerushalmi Fragments from the Genizah. I. Text with various readings from the editio princeps.* 1909. Reprint, New York and Hildesheim: Georg Olms Verlag, 1970.

Git.: Gittin.

GRA: Elijah b. Solomon Zalman ("HaGaon Rabbi Eliyahu," or "Vilna Gaon," Lithuania, 1720–97). Mishnah commentary, in Romm edition of Mishnah.

Habdalah: The ceremony which marks the conclusion of a sabbath or festival and the beginning of an ordinary day.

Haber: A person who (1) separates all required agricultural offerings from food he grows or purchases, and (2) eats his food in a state of cultic cleanness.

Hag.: Hagigah.

Hal.: Hallah.

Halisah: The ceremony which severs the bond between a man and the widow of his brother who has died childless (see Deut. 25:7–9).

Hallel: A portion of the liturgy consisting of Pss. 113–18, recited on festivals and new moons.

Halusah: A woman who has undergone the ceremony of *halisah*.

Haroset: A relish made of fruits and spices with vinegar or wine, used to sweeten the bitter herb at the Passover meal (see M. Pes. 10:3).

Herem: Something set aside for use of the priests or Temple. The term is used in vows of abstinence, by which an individual prohibits himself from use of a named object.

Holy Things: Jacob Neusner. *A History of the Mishnaic Law of Holy Things.* 6 vols. Leiden: E. J. Brill, 1978–79.

Hor.: Horayot.

Hul.: Hullin.

Isa.: Isaiah.

Issar: A coin valued at one-forty-eighth of a *shekel.*

Issaron: A measure of volume equal to one-tenth of an ephah.

Jastrow: Marcus Jastrow. *A Dictionary of the Targumim, the Talmud Babli and Yerushalmi, and the Midrashic Literature.* 2 vols. Reprint, New York: Pardes Publishing House, 1950.

Jer.: Jeremiah.

Josh.: Joshua.

Karmelit: An area of land classified neither as public nor private domain.

Kel.: Kelim.

Ker.: Keritot.

Kerem rebai: A vineyard in its fourth year of growth, the produce of which is deemed sanctified (see Lev. 19:24).

Ket.: Ketubot.

Ketubah: A marriage contract indicating the sum of money due to the wife upon her husband's death or on being divorced.

Kil.: Kilayim.

Kor: A dry measure.

Koy: An animal about which there is a doubt whether it is in the category of domesticated or undomesticated beasts.

Krauss: Samuel Krauss. *Griechische und Lateinische Lehnwörter im Talmud, Midrasch, und Targum.* 1899. Reprint, Hildesheim: Georg Olms Verlagsbuchhandlung, 1964.

Lam.: Lamentations.

Leiden MS: *The Palestinian Talmud. Leiden MS. Cod Scal. 3. A Facsimile of the original manuscript.* 4 vols. Introduction by Saul Lieberman. Jerusalem, Kedem Publishing: 1970.

Letekh: A measure of volume, equal to one and one-half ephah.

Lev.: Leviticus.

Lieberman, Caesarea: Saul Lieberman. *The Talmud of Caesarea. Jerushalmi Tractate Nezikin.* Jerusalem, 1931. *Supplement to Tarbiz* II.4. In Hebrew.

Lieberman, TR: Saul Lieberman. *Tosefeth Rishonim. A Commentary. Based on Manuscripts of the Tosefta and Works of the Rishonim and Midrashim in Manuscripts and Rare Editions.* Jerusalem: Mossad Rabbi Kook Press, 1939. (In Hebrew).

Lieberman[n], YK: Saul Lieberman[n]. *HaYerushalmi Kiphshuto. A Commentary based on manuscripts of the Yerushalmi and works of the Rishonim and Midrashim in Mss. and rare editions.* Jerusalem: Darom Publishing Co., 1934. I, i *Sabbath, Erubin, Pesahim.* (In Hebrew.)

Litra: A measure of volume equal to $\frac{1}{144}$ of an ephah.

Log: One-seventy-second of an ephah.

Lulab: The branches of palm, myrtle, and willow which are bound together and carried along with the *etrog* on the Festival of Boothes (see Lev. 23:40).

M.: Mishnah.

Ma.: Maaserot.

Maah: A coin valued at one-twelfth *shekel*.

Maamad: A priestly course, that is, one of the twenty-four groups of priests from districts outside of Jerusalem. These served in the Temple in rotation.

Maddaf: The level of uncleanness conveyed by a *zab* or *zabah* to an object which is located above his head.

Mak.: Makkot.

Makh.: Makhshirin.

Mal.: Malachi.

Mamzer(et): The offspring of a man and woman who could not legally marry one another.

Maneh: A weight of gold or silver equal to fifty *shekel*s.

Markof: The name of a musical instrument.

Marshall: J. T. Marshall. *Manual of the Aramaic Language of the Palestinian Talmud. Grammar, vocalized text, translation, and vocabulary.* Ed. J. Barton Turner. With introduction by A. Mingana Leiden: E. J. Brill, 1929.

Me.: Meilah.

Meg.: Megillah.

Melammed: E. Z. Melammed. *An Introduction to Talmudic Literature.* Jerusalem, 1973. (In Hebrew.)

Melog: Property owned by one individual (usually a wife) the in-come from which accrues to a different person (the husband).

Men.: Menahot.

Mesora: A person unclean with the disease referred to at Lev. 13:3ff.

Mezuzah: A strip of parchment inscribed with Deut. 6:4–9 and 11:18–21. In accordance with Deut. 6:9 it is fastened to the doorpost of an Israelite's house. Pl.: *mezuzot*.

Mid.: Middot.

Midras-uncleanness: The level of uncleanness conveyed by any of the individuals listed at Lev. 12:2, 15:2, 25, to objects on which they exert pressure.

Mil: Two thousand cubits.

Min.: A heretic (pl.: *minim*).

Miq.: Miqvaot.

Moshav: The level of impurity conveyed by an unclean person to a chair or other object normally used for sitting.

M.Q.: Moed Qatan.

M.S.: Maaser Sheni.

MᶜSH B (W): A formulaic phrase used to introduce a legal precedent.

Naz.: Nazir.

Nazirite: One who has taken a vow neither to cut his hair, drink wine, nor contract corpse-uncleanness (see Num. 6:1–27).

Ned.: Nedarim.

Neg.: Negaim.

Nega: A sore on the body which may indicate that the individual is unclean with the disease *saraat*, referred to at Lev. 13:3ff.

Neh.: Nehemiah.

Netin(ah): A descendant of the Gibeonites, designated at Josh. 9:27 as Temple slaves. They have impaired status within the Israelite community (see M. Qid. 4:1ff).

Nid.: Niddah.

Niddah: A woman unclean through menstruation.

Num.: Numbers.

NY: *Noam Yerushalmi.* Joshua Isaac Salonima. *Sefer Noam Yerushalmi. Vehu beur al hayyerushalmi.* 2 vols. Vilna, 1868. Reprint, Jerusalem, 1968.

Oh.: Ohalot.

Omer: The first sheaf of the season, which must be harvested and offered in the Temple as a meal offering. Only when this is done may the rest of the new grain be reaped (Lev. 23:10).

Or.: Orlah.

Orlah: Produce from an orchard in its first three years of growth, which may not be eaten (see Lev. 19:23).

'P: A formulaic word used to introduce a named authority's expansion of a preceding rule.

Par.: Parah.

Parvah-chamber: The name of a particular room in the Temple.

Pe.: Peah.

Peah: Produce which grows in the corner of the field and must be left unharvested, to be collected by the poor (see Lev. 19:9ff).

PM: Moses Margolies (d. 1780). *Pené Moshe.* Amsterdam, 1754; Leghorn, 1770. Reprinted in Y.

Perutah: A copper coin of small denomination.

Pes.: Pesahim.

Pondion: One-twenty-fourth of a *shekel.*

Prayer: The Eighteen Benedictions.

Prov.: Proverbs.

Prozbul: The legal document which allows creditors to circumvent the usual abolition of debts in the seventh year of the sabbatical cycle (see M. Sheb. 10:4). The debts are assigned to a court, which prevents their being remitted.

Ps.: Psalms.

Pundium: One-sixth of a *shekel.*

Purities: Jacob Neusner. *A History of the Mishnaic Law of Purities.* 12 vols. Leiden: E. J. Brill, 1974–77.

Qab: A measure of volume equal to one-eighteenth of an ephah.

Qal vehomer: An argument *a minori ad majus.*

Qartob: A liquid or dry measure, equal to one-sixty-fourth of a *log.*

QE: Elijah of Fulda. *Qorban Ha'edah.* Dessau, 1743; Berlin, 1757, 1760–62. Reprinted in Y.

Qid.: Qiddushin.

Qin.: Qinnim.

R.: Rabbi.

Rabbinowitz: Louis I. Rabbinowitz. "Talmud, Jerusalem." In *Encyclopaedia Judaica* (Jerusalem, 1971), 15:772–79.

Rabinovitz, STEI: Z. W. Rabinovitz. *Sha'are Torath Eretz Israel. Notes and Comments on Yeru-*

shalmi. Jerusalem, 1940; Published by his son.

Ratner: B. Ratner. *Ahawath Zion we-Jeruscholaim. Varianten und Ergänzungen des Textes des Jerusalemitischen Talmuds nach alten Quellen und handschriftlichen Fragmenten ediert, mit kritischen Noten und Erläuterungen versehen.* Vilna: Wittwe & Gebr. Romm *et al.* I, *Berakhot* (1901); II, *Shabbat* (1902); III, *Terumot, Hallah* (1904); IV, *Shebiᶜit* (1905); V, *Kilayim, Maᶜaserot* (1907); VI, *Pesahim* (1908); VII, *Yoma* (1909); VIII, *Rosh Hashshanah, Sukkah* (1911); IX, *Megillah* (1912); X, *Besah, Taanit* (1913); XII, *Peʾah Demai, Maᶜaser Sheni, ᶜOrlah, Bikkurim* (1917). No number: *Sheqalim, Hagigah, Moᶜed Qatan.* Jerusalem, 1967.

Regel: One of the three pilgrimage festivals, Passover, Pentecost, Booths (Tabernacles). (Pl.: *regalim.*)

R.H.: Rosh Hashshanah.

Sam.: Samuel.

San.: Sanhedrin.

Schwab: Moïse Schwab. *Le Talmud de Jérusalem. Traduit pour la première fois en français.* Reprint, Paris, 1960.

Seah: One-third of an ephah.

Sela: A small coin.

Shaatnez: Fabric in which wool and linen are woven together. This is forbidden under the law of Diverse Kinds.

Shab.: Shabbat.

Shabu.: Shabuot.

Shebuah: An oath.

Shekel: The chief silver coin of the Israelites, weighing between one-quarter and one-half of an ounce.

Shema: A section of the liturgy composed of Deut. 6:4–9, 11:13–21, and Num. 15:37–41. It is recited twice daily, morning and evening.

Sheq.: Sheqalim.

Shittuf: A deposit of food placed jointly by neighbors sharing a courtyard in order to transform all of their homes into a single, collective domain for purposes of carrying burdens on the Sabbath. Cf. *Erub.*

Shofar: A ram's horn, blown on set occasions in Temple and synagogue worship.

Sit: The distance between the extended thumb and index finger.

Sot.: Sotah.

Suk.: Sukkah.

Sukkah: A temporary dwelling ("booth") in which Israelites live during the Festival of Tabernacles, in fulfillment of Lev. 34–36, 39–43.

Sukkot: Tabernacles.

T.: Tosefta.

Ta.: Taanit.

Tam.: Tamid.

Tebul-yom: A person who has immersed in a ritual bath and awaits the setting of the sun, which marks the completion of the process of purification.

Tefillin: Phylacteries, tied on head and arm, containing the four passages: Ex. 13:1–10, 11–16, Deut. 6:4–9, 11:13–21.

Tem.: Temurah.

Teqiah: A blast of a *shofar*.

Ter.: Terumot.

Terefah: Meat which is ruined in the process of ritual slaughter through some improper act of the slaughterer.

Terisit: A coin.

Toh.: Tohorot.

Tumtom: One whose sex is indistinguishable.

T.Y.: Tebul Yom.

Uqs.: Uqsin.

Women: Jacob Neusner. *A History of the Mishnaic Law of Women.* 5 vols. Leiden: E. J. Brill, 1979–80.

Y: Yerushalmi, Talmud of the Land of Israel.

Yad.: Yadayyim.

Yeb.: Yebamot.

Yom.: Yoma.

Y.T.: Yom Tob.

Zab.: Zabim.

Zab/zabah: A person who has suffered a flux and is deemed unclean. Pl.: *zabim, zabot*.

Zeb.: Zebahim.

Zech.: Zechariah.

Zuckermandel: M. S. Zuckermandel. *Tosephta. Based on the Erfurt and Vienna Codices with parallels and variants.* (Reprint, Jerusalem: Wahrmann Books, 1963.

Zuz: A coin valued at a *denar* (i.e., one-half of a *shekel*). Pl.: *zuzim*.

Index of Biblical and Talmudic References

General Index

Abba b. Daliah, inheritances and wills, 134
Abba bar Hanah, inheritances and wills, 144
Abba bar Jeremiah, inheritances and wills, 157
Abbahu: buildings, obligation of contractors, 114; debts, validating of, 179, 186; infringing property rights of others, 47–48; inheritances and wills, 160; sales, liability of seller, 110, 114; security bonds, 189; usucaption, title by, 55
Abba Saul, infringing property rights of others, 46, 51
Abbaye, infringing property rights of others, 48
Abedomi: infringing property rights of others, 40; inheritances and wills, 155; squatters' rights, 56
Abimi bar Tobi, infringing property rights of others, 42
Abin, debts, validation of, 180
Ada bar Abbahu, squatters' rights, 53
Admon: inheritances and wills, 153, 157; property, conditions of sales, 81–82
Aha: debts, validation of, 186; infringing property rights of others, 39–40; inheritances and wills, 127, 169; security bonds, 190–191
Ami: debts, validation of, 186; inheritances and wills, 164, 163; squatters' rights, 54
Ami bar Qorha, security bonds, 190
Ammi, inheritances and wills, 145, 161
Aqiba: buildings, obligation of contractors, 113; debts, validation of, 182; infringing property rights of others, 47; inheritances and wills, 171, 174; joint ownership, lia-

bilities, 31; land sales, measurements for, 121; property, conditions for sales, 80–82, 87, 90, 97; sales, liability of seller, 113, 121; squatters' rights, 58–59

Ba: debts, validation of, 176–177, 180, 184–185; inheritances and wills, 127; squatters' rights, 57, 61, 64
Ba Bar Mamal: inheritances and wills, 140, 142; property, conditions of sales, 104
Ba Bar Tabelai, property, conditions of sales, 89
Ba bar Zabeda, inheritances and wills, 157
Bailment, liability for, 11–12, 14–15
Bar Qappara: joint ownership, liabilities, 32; squatters' rights, 54
Benaiah, joint ownership, liabilities, 32
Ben Azzai: debts, validation of, 182; inheritances and wills, 174
Ben Nannos, security bonds, 192–193
Buildings, obligations of contractors, 20–21, 113–114
Bun, inheritances and wills, 170
Bun bar Hiyya: property, conditions of sales, 105; sales, liability of seller, 108
Bun bar Kahana: inheritances and wills, 147; sales, liability of seller, 109

Chattels causing damage, 3–7
Commercial dealings, overcharges and misrepresentation, 12–13

Debts, validation of, 22–23, 175, 188
Dosetai b. Judah, inheritances and wills, 132
Dosetai b. R. Yannai, debts, validation of, 178